People are asking

IS THIS THE END?

Signs of God's Providence in a Disturbing New World

STUDY GUIDE

TEN SESSIONS

DR. DAVID JEREMIAH

W PUBLISHING GROUP

AN IMPRINT OF THOMAS NELSON

thomasnelson.com

© 2016 David P. Jeremiah
Box 3838, San Diego, CA 92163
All Rights Reserved

Published in Nashville, Tennessee, by W Publishing, an imprint of Thomas Nelson. W Publishing and Thomas Nelson are registered trademarks of HarperCollins Christian Publishing, Inc.

Published in association with Yates & Yates, LLP, www.yates2.com.

All Scripture quotations, unless otherwise indicated, are taken from the *New King James Version*. Copyright © 1982 by Thomas Nelson. Used by permission. All rights reserved.

Scripture quotations marked NIV taken from the New International Version®, NIV®. Copyright © 1973, 1978, 1984, 2011 by Biblica, Inc.® Used by permission. All rights reserved worldwide.

Edited by William Kruidenier

Thomas Nelson titles may be purchased in bulk for educational, business, fund-raising, or sales promotional use. For information, please e-mail SpecialMarkets@ThomasNelson.com.

ISBN 978-0-310-08618-5

First printing September 2016 / Printed in the United States of America

Contents

About This Study Guide

The purpose of this study guide is to reinforce Dr. David Jeremiah's dynamic, in-depth teaching and to aid the reader in applying biblical truth to his or her daily life. This study guide is designed to be used in conjunction with Dr. Jeremiah's *People Are Asking . . . Is This the End?* trade book and audio series, but it may also be used by itself for personal or group study.

STRUCTURE OF THE LESSONS

Each lesson is based on one of the messages in the *People Are Asking . . . Is This the End?* audio series and trade book and focuses on specific passages in the Bible. Each lesson is composed of the following elements:

- **Outline:** The outline at the beginning of the lesson gives a clear, concise picture of the topic being studied and provides a helpful framework for readers as they listen to Dr. Jeremiah's teaching or read the trade book.

- **Overview:** The overview summarizes Dr. Jeremiah's teaching on the passage being studied in the lesson. Readers should refer to the Scripture passages in their own Bibles as they study the overview. Unless otherwise indicated, Scripture verses quoted are taken from the *New King James Version*.

- **Application:** This section contains a variety of questions designed to help readers dig deeper into the lesson and the Scriptures and to apply the lesson to their daily lives. For Bible study groups or Sunday school classes, these questions will provide a springboard for group discussion and interaction.

- **Did You Know?** This section presents a fascinating fact, historical note, or insight that adds a point of interest to the preceding lesson.

USING THIS GUIDE FOR GROUP STUDY

The lessons in this study guide are suitable for Sunday school classes, small-group studies, elective Bible studies, or home Bible study groups. Each person in the group should have his or her own study guide.

When possible, the study guide should be used with the corresponding audio series. You may wish to assign the study guide lesson as homework prior to the meeting of the group and then use the meeting time to listen to Dr. Jeremiah's teaching and discuss the lesson.

FOR CONTINUING STUDY

For a complete listing of Dr. Jeremiah's materials for personal and group study, call 1-800-947-1993, go online to www.DavidJeremiah.org, or write to Turning Point, P.O. Box 3838, San Diego, CA 92163.

Dr. Jeremiah's *Turning Point* program is currently heard or viewed around the world on radio, television, and the Internet in English. *Momento Decisivo*, the Spanish translation of Dr. Jeremiah's messages, can be heard on radio in every Spanish speaking country in the world. The television broadcast is also broadcast by satellite throughout the Middle East with Arabic subtitles.

Contact Turning Point for radio and television program times and stations in your area. Or visit our website at www.DavidJeremiah.org.

Is This the End?

The title of Dr. David Jeremiah's series, and the title of this accompanying study guide—*Is This the End?*—could have been plucked right from the daily headlines. The entire title—*People Are Asking . . . Is This the End?*—says it all. People are trying to understand the crises erupting all around the world. From terrorism to natural disasters to political upheavals to refugees to disease to nuclear threats to failing economies . . . and the list goes on. Never before have so many worldwide events developed so quickly and with such catastrophic implications. People are, in fact, asking, "Is this the end?"

Jesus Christ said it was vanity to theorize about the exact time of the end of the age (Mark 13:31–33). But we do know there will be "birth pangs" as all of creation labors under the effects of sin, laboring to give birth to new heavens and a new earth (Romans 8:22). Are we approaching the end of the age?

This series and study guide can't answer that question specifically. The purpose of this series is to step back from the trees and look at the forest. To swap our daily micro-view that we get from the media and take a macro-view at what is happening in the world. To do that, Dr. Jeremiah focuses on ten developments that signal a significant shift in the moral, spiritual, and geo-political landscape of our world and the United States.

The ten developments are divided equally into two parts: "Is This the End for America?" and "Is This the End for the World?" Each is explained and evaluated from a biblical perspective.

The first part explains five developments taking place in America:

1. **"The Age of Anything Goes":** Looks at the devolving moral standards in America. Our nation has lost her moral compass and is adrift.
2. **"The Bleeding of Our Borders":** Tackles the divisive issue of immigration from a biblical and practical point of view.

3. **"The Increase of Intolerance"**: Examines how those who believe in Christ have become the most persecuted group in America. Christianity has been moved out of the mainstream of the culture in both politics and the marketplace.

4. **"The Apathy of America"**: Studies America's founding and past blessings, our present loss of God's favor, and possible scenarios for America's future.

5. **"The Remedy of Revival"**: Reviews the historical revivals that kept America from sinking into immorality and apostasy—and how revival could yet rescue America again.

The second part explains five developments taking place around the world:

6. **"The Isolation of Israel"**: The nation where God's chosen people are coming back together is both prosperous and persecuted. What does the future hold for the world's most important people?

7. **"The Insurgency of ISIS"**: The recent insurgency of ISIS on the world stage, with ancient roots in Middle Eastern racial and religious tensions, epitomizes radical Islamic militancy. Their goal of a worldwide Islamic government means those outside the Middle East must be cautiously aware of their intentions.

8. **"The Resurrection of Russia"**: The nation that was almost irrelevant following the dissolution of the Soviet Union has come roaring back. Russia will play a significant role in end-time events.

9. **"The Rapture of the Redeemed"**: The next event on God's prophetic calendar—the removal of the Church before the start of the seven-year Tribulation.

10. **"Translated Before the Tribulation"**: The one event that no right-thinking person on earth should want to be around for. What it is and how to avoid it.

This series and study guide will equip you to understand some of the shifts happening in our world today—and to make spiritual preparations for whatever comes.

PART I

Is This the End for America?

The Age of Anything Goes

ROMANS 1:18–32

This lesson defines the issues playing a role in our culture today and offers insights into how the Christian can make a difference in an age where "anything goes."

OUTLINE

We live in a time that is historically unprecedented in its open idolatry, debauchery, and pursuit of immorality, but as we look to God's Word we gain understanding on how to live for Christ during a time of moral decline.

I. The Expression of Our Moral Decline
    A. Depravity in Our Minds
    B. Depravity in Our Marriages
    C. Depravity in Our Military
    D. Depravity in Medicine

II. The Explanation of Our Moral Decline
    A. The Historical Explanation
    B. The Biblical Explanation

OVERVIEW

We live in an age of decadence, where the shameful acts of yesterday are the celebrated triumphs of today. Perversions are seen as normal, purity is labeled as puritanical, and the pursuit of personal pleasure is king. As Christians we should not be surprised at the depths to which humanity continues to sink because Scripture clearly speaks of man's propensity to sin and God's holy intolerance of it. It is no wonder that we have found ourselves in a place where "anything goes."

"Anything Goes" is the memorable toe-tapping song written by Cole Porter in 1934. If you listen closely to the lyrics you will find they celebrate the moral free fall of the American twentieth century. "We've rewound the clock," say the lyrics. Profanity and nudity are in vogue, and "now God knows—anything goes."

"Anything Goes" represents the moral relativism that has infected our culture, leaving the West on the brink of spiritual collapse. Ironically, it's a philosophy that ruined Cole Porter's own life. His secretary lamented that her boss never found the strength that came from faith in God. We're living in a world where anything goes, but nothing satisfies. That is why it is vital for Christ-followers to resist the siren calls of our decadent age.

The Expression of Our Moral Decline

The Bible anticipated these times. In speaking about His Second Coming, the Lord Jesus said, "But of that day and hour no one knows, not even the angels of heaven, but My Father only. For as the days of Noah were, so also will the coming of the Son of Man be" (Matthew 24:36–37).

Those words take us back to Genesis 6:5, which is a description of the society swept away by the flood: "Then the LORD saw that the wickedness of man was great in the earth, and that every intent of the thoughts of his heart was only evil continually."

Read 2 Timothy 3:1–5, where we are reminded "that in the last days perilous times will come: For men will be lovers of themselves . . . without self-control, brutal, despisers of good . . . lovers of pleasure rather than lovers of God, having a form of godliness, but denying its power."

This rejection of God and His standards is a symptom of our isolation from God. It began at the Fall of man and continues to this day. Depravity is the root cause of America's moral decline.

Depravity in Our Minds

The Internet offers many benefits for us today, but it created an avenue for destructive behavior that is staggering in its reach: pornography. Online pornography is an addictive and destructive trap that brings lurid material into the hearts and souls of consumers. Even worse, over one quarter of Internet pornography is child related.[1] It is a sickening trend, which brings with it a depravity of the mind and soul, with innocent children being abused—causing emotional scars that last a lifetime. Sexually explicit content is not limited to the Internet; television today contains material that in earlier decades would have never been allowed. There are not adequate words to describe the sex, violence, and addictive nature of some of today's options for so-called entertainment.

In Noah's day, every thought was only of evil continually, but today we have the technology to take the most lurid fantasies of the human mind and project them onto a screen a child or adult can hold in his or her hand.

All this has led to the coarsening of Western culture. We've become a profane people, with fewer restraints on behavior and language, and with a lessening respect for human life, even innocent life in the womb.

Depravity in Our Marriages

Another aspect of our sexually demanding society is vehemence of the LGBTQ movement (lesbian, gay, bisexual, transgender, questioning), which won a great legal victory in 2015. In the case of Obergefell v. Hodges, the Supreme Court of the United States, in a 5-to-4 vote, took it upon itself to "redefine" marriage.

But God Himself defined the marriage covenant in Genesis 2, in the Garden of Eden, before human governments were established. It wasn't human government, Mosaic Law, or church councils that established the definition of marriage. God did it before any of those institutions came into existence.

The Lord established the formula for marriage just like He established the law of gravity or the axioms of physics. God ordained marriage as a lifelong covenant union between one man and one woman, and this is the only proper God-given arena for the exercise of sexual relations.

Depravity in Our Military

Today, Bible-believing members of our Armed Forces face new restrictions on expressing their religion, and our military chaplains are on the front lines of intense pressure to be politically correct. While at this point there is no official policy banning voluntary prayer, religious services, or pastoral counseling, there have been several instances where Christian chaplains have run into politically correct buzz saws for praying in Jesus' name, counseling from a Christian perspective, and expressing biblical standards for sexuality.

We have yet to see the full moral effect of the U.S. military's recent policies of allowing gays to serve in the military and the inclusion of women in combat roles. But it should be clear to any objective thinker that these decisions cannot but foster increased moral deterioration, not to mention diluting the effectiveness of our forces in combat.

Depravity in Medicine

Dr. Paul Church is one of Boston's most-loved physicians, a urologist who invested 28 years practicing medicine at Beth Israel Deaconess Medical Center and teaching at Harvard University. One day, hospital officials noticed that on the hospital's online portal, Dr. Church had posted concern about the health dangers of same-sex activity.

In September 2014, the hospital launched a formal investigation into Dr. Church's views, and that began a long and losing battle for Dr. Church, who has now been expelled from the hospital.[2] Sadly, we have reached the point where political correctness trumps public health concerns. As the Bible puts it: "For the time will come when people will not put up with sound doctrine. Instead, to suit their own desires, they will gather around them a great number of teachers to say what their itching ears want to hear. They will turn their ears away from the truth and turn aside to myths" (2 Timothy 4:3–4 NIV).

The Explanation of Our Moral Decline

It's time to ask the question: How did Western morality arrive on such a slippery slope? What happened to us? It can be explained in two ways: (1) historically; and (2) biblically.

The Historical Explanation

The historical explanation dates back to the eighteenth century Enlightenment. Throughout the Middle Ages, the Western world, for all its darkness and depravity, at least had an understanding of objective truth. The existence of God was granted, which provided a basis for belief in absolute values of right and wrong. But hard on the heels of the Reformation, the secular thinking of the Enlightenment (or the Age of Reason) radiated from France like a force field across Europe and to the New World.

As philosophy detached itself from religion, morality was liberated from divine authority. This newfound "freedom" and doctrine of the perfectibility of humanity set the stage for all kinds of mischief—the Communist movement of Karl Marx, the theological liberalism of Julius Wellhausen, and the evolutionary hypotheses of Charles Darwin.

Darwin's evolutionary ideas spread to all other areas of thought, including non-scientific philosophical arenas. We are constantly changing and forever evolving, said the enlightened thinkers, and that includes our values. Darwinian morality replaced biblical codes of conduct and character.

The rising tide of humanistic secularism was shoehorned into America's education system by John Dewey, a shy, bookish educator who hailed from Vermont. Dewey's core principle was the rejection of absolute unchangeable truth. Final truth, he believed, was illusionary.[3]

About that time, the American judicial system entered the picture and began mandating secularism, almost as though it were the nation's new official religion. In 1963, the Supreme Court of the United States prohibited school officials from organizing or leading Bible reading or prayer exercises in schools. We've now had two generations to see how that has worked out.

Against this backdrop, moral relativism entered the pop culture with a vengeance between the 1920s and 1960s—remember, Cole Porter wrote "Anything Goes" in 1934—and set the stage for the sexual revolution of the 1960s through the 1980s. Hollywood jumped on the bandwagon, and

America's moral values turned downward like economic charts of the Great Depression. The culture today is reaping the seeds of moral relativism and a secular world view.

The Biblical Explanation

While we can trace the philosophical decline of our moral foundations, the true explanation is found in humanity's rebellion against the holy character of God.

A culture begins to collapse, said Paul, when it rejects the reality of creationism and of a Creator. Romans 1:18–20 says, "For the wrath of God is revealed from heaven against all the ungodliness and unrighteousness of men, who suppress the truth in unrighteousness, because what may be known of God is manifest in them, for God has shown it to them. For since the creation of the world His invisible attributes are clearly seen, being understood in the things that are made, even His eternal power and Godhead, so that they are without excuse."

The existence and complexity of Creation demands a Designer. This presents an insolvable problem for modern humanity, for the existence of a Creator implies His authority over all His creation. If we're subject to a Maker, we're not autonomous, for morality is intrinsically rooted in His holy character.

To escape these implications, our society has chosen to believe the unbelievable—that everything came from nothing in an unexplainable explosion, that primordial sludge was jolted from death to life, that molecules developed from randomness into complexity, and that human beings are the resulting accidents. That's the foundation of secularism, and it leads downward in belief and behavior. It leads to ingratitude.

We Have Rejected God Through Ingratitude

Paul wrote, "because, although they knew God, they did not glorify Him as God, nor were *thankful*, but became futile in their thoughts, and their foolish hearts were darkened" (Romans 1:21, italics added).

We Have Rejected God Through Idolatry

The rejection of the Creator-God means only one thing—humanity must construct its own gods. Romans 1:22–23 goes on to say, "Professing to be wise, they became fools, and changed the glory of the incorruptible God into an image made like corruptible man."

Anything that comes before Jesus Christ in your affections or priorities—that's your idol. In Colossians 3:5, the apostle Paul told his readers, "Therefore put to death your members which are on the earth: fornication, uncleanness, passion, evil desire, and covetousness, which is idolatry."

Our goals, ambitions, dreams, obsessions, addictions, pleasures, or opinions can become our gods. But make no mistake—when we reject the Creator-God of Scripture, we must find a substitute. We must have an idol, which leads to the next downward step—a lust-driven life.

We Have Rejected God Through Immorality

Paul continues in Romans 1:24–25 to say, "Therefore God also gave them up to the uncleanness, in the lusts of their hearts, to dishonor their bodies among themselves, who exchanged the truth of God for the lie, and worshiped and served the creature rather than the Creator, who is blessed forever. Amen."

Only the true God of heaven is holy enough to empower His people to live according to the dictates of His holiness. All other gods lead to an erosion of morality, to sensuality, to sexual sins, and to lust-driven lives. How sad to follow this downward course when God longs to give us an upward path. But the steps keep descending. The next stop on the way to the days of Noah is a sex-saturated society.

We Have Rejected God Through Iniquity

When a culture denies its Creator, erects its own gods, and succumbs to a lust-driven existence, it inevitably becomes sex-saturated. Romans 1:26–27 says plainly: "For this reason God gave them up to vile passions. For even their women exchanged the natural use of what is against nature. Likewise also the men, leaving the natural use of the woman, burned in their lust for one another, men with men committing what is shameful, and receiving in themselves the penalty of their error which was due."

This downward spiral of decency finally leads to the basement of debauchery—total moral collapse.

The history of the world is littered with the stories of cultures who descended this staircase never to return. Our pathway from the Enlightenment to Postmodernism isn't new. The same thing happened in the days of Noah. It happened to Sodom and Gomorrah. It happened to the ancient empires of Assyria, Babylon, Greece, and Rome. It even happened to ancient Judah in the days of the prophet Ezekiel.

The Lord's glory dwelt in His Temple for 400 years. But by the time of King Zedekiah, however, the temple of the Lord was a different place, for the nation of Judah had followed step-by-step the sequence of sin described in Romans 1: the rejection of the Creator, the proliferation of idols, lust-driven hearts, a sexually saturated age, that led to total moral collapse.

As the Babylonians began their assault on Judah, one of the early victims was Ezekiel. In chapters 8–11 of his book, Ezekiel described how he was given the awful privilege of watching the glory depart from Judah. The biblical word for this is *Ichabod*—the glory has departed. All hope for Israel was gone—decimated by the Babylonians. But before you despair that *Ichabod* may now be indelibly inscribed on America, let me give you hope. In lesson 5 we will learn the story of revivals that have saved our nation in the past.

The Church of Jesus Christ and its message are the only things standing between this world and the judgment of God. Our Lord has placed us here for times like these, and we mustn't be drawn into the corruption of our culture. Instead, we're to shine like stars in the nighttime as we firmly hold out the Word of life to a crumbling culture (Philippians 2:15–16).

The Bible tells us to remain fully committed to Christ, to keep ourselves unspotted from the world, to hold our convictions without fear, and to preach the Gospel without compromise. It's easy to condemn our age—and we certainly have the biblical authority to speak the truth and expose sin—but we also need to demonstrate Christ to our world.

Without succumbing to the ways of the world, we should reach out in love to the people of the world, reflecting the heart of Christ to everyone we meet. Let's remember the truth of John 3:16—despite everything, God loves this world.

Our times are not lost on our Lord. He understands our culture, and He loves its people. We're engaged in our times because Jesus died for times like these, and we are living in a world for which He offered Himself on the cross.

I hope you feel as I do, that it's an honor to represent Jesus Christ to my generation, even in times like these. It's an honor to be a light in a darkened age.

Keep yourself unspotted from the world, but don't disengage from the world. Let's love our neighbors and rescue the perishing. We are here in these days as His ambassadors on assignment, serving the One who told us to go into all the world with the Gospel—even into a world where "anything goes."

APPLICATION

I. Read Genesis 6:1–8.

    a. What were the conditions on earth like as defined in verse 5?

    b. Describe the implications of the words "every" and "only" in verse 5.

    c. Verse 6 mentions two reactions that God had to this situation. What were they?

    d. What was God's plan of action in the face of this (verse 7)? Why?

    e. What do you think the purpose of verse 8 is in light of the preceding passage?

2. Read Romans 2:1–11.

    a. According to verse 1, what can be said of those who judge? Why is that?

    b. How does God judge (verse 2)?

c. What are the implications of verse 3, especially for Christians living today?

d. What does God's goodness lead to (verse 4)? Why do you think that is?

e. What two attributes build up the wrath of God against you (verse 5)?

f. When will this come to fruition?

g. To whom is eternal life bestowed (verse 7)?

h. List the four results of living a disobedient, self-seeking life (verses 8–9).

i. To whom will this occur? Be specific (verses 8–9).

j. What three things come to those who work for good (verse 10)?

k. Rephrase verse 11 in your own words and then explain how it relates to this study.

3. Read Romans 2:12–16.

a. Explain how it is possible to sin "without law" and "perish without law."

b. Why is it that the doers and not the hearers of the law are justified as stated in verse 13?

c. What, according to verse 15, bears witness to the law in the unbeliever's heart? What is the implication of this reality?

d. What will God judge one day? How (verse 16)?

e. What kind of material and ideas has Romans 2:1–16 given you that can aid you in approaching nonbelievers with the truth of God's Word? What have you learned about the inner working of unbelievers from this passage?

DID YOU KNOW?

The Scopes Trial of 1925 was a landmark event and the biggest trial of the Roaring Twenties. The ACLU wanted to try a case against the Butler Act, a Tennessee Law that banned the teaching of evolution in state-funded schools. They found a willing participant in a small town teacher by the name of John Scopes, and financed a trial that featured two of the most prominent lawyers in America, William Jennings Bryan and Clarence Darrow. This trial set the stage for future conflicts where state-funded schools would teach evolution in defiance of previously established biblical standards.

Notes
1. Cited by Harry Leibowitz, World of Children Award Co-Founder and Board Chairman, in "The Numbers: Child Sexual Imposition in the United States," *Huffington Post*, February 12, 2016, www.huffingtonpost.com/harry-leibowitz/ the-numbers-child-sexual-_b_9101508.html.
2. "Doc Faces Boot for Citing 'Gay,' *Health Dangers*," June 27, 2015, in http://www.wnd.com/2015/06/doc-faces-boot-for-citing-gay-health-dangers/.
3. David Breese, *Seven Men Who Rule the World from the Grave* (Chicago: Moody, 1990), 170.

LESSON 2

The Bleeding of Our Borders

SELECTED SCRIPTURES

In this lesson we look at the subject of immigration
through the lens of Scripture.

OUTLINE

As of 2016, the problem of refugees and undocumented immigrants is broached almost daily in the American and international news cycles. Christians are torn between compassion toward strangers in our midst and an obligation to obey civil laws. What is the biblical perspective?

I. The Potential of Immigration

II. The Problems with Immigration
   A. Problems with Legal Immigration
   B. Problems with Illegal Immigration

III. The Past of Immigration

IV. The Principles of Immigration
   A. God's People Are to Assist the Stranger
   B. God's People Are to Accept the Stranger
   C. God's People Are to Assimilate the Stranger

V. The Perfection of Immigration

OVERVIEW

Immigration has become a hot political and social issue creating sharp division in the United States. But historically, immigration has been part of our national DNA. Our nation's historic attitude toward immigrants is eloquently expressed in the poetic words of Emma Lazarus engraved on the pedestal of the Statue of Liberty: "Give me your tired, your poor, your huddled masses yearning to breathe free, the wretched refuse of your teeming shore. Send these, the homeless, tempest-tost to me, I lift my lamp beside the golden door!"

American immigration began with the Puritans in the early 1600s who sought religious freedom. Then, over two centuries, hundreds of thousands of Africans were forcibly brought to America as slaves. From 1820 through 2010, the United States attracted eighty million newcomers—sixty percent of all the world's immigrants. And the rate has ballooned in the twenty-first century with almost fourteen million arriving between 2000 and 2010.[1]

In the last few decades, the pattern of immigration in America has shifted: fewer from Europe, more from the Middle East and Asia, and the largest segment from Latin America, especially Mexico. The hot-button issue in America regarding immigration at present is the number of undocumented (illegal) immigrants, which is estimated at thirteen million. What to do about undocumented immigrants is a divisive issue in America.

The Potential of Immigration

Americans love the diversity of cultures, food, music, and even holidays that result from centuries of immigration. People not born in the United States now make up large proportions of small business owners. Multitudes of immigrants also work as gardeners, nannies, cooks, policemen, maids, teachers, farm workers, construction workers, entertainers, and athletes.

But there is another way immigrants are impacting our society: spiritually. In a day when American Christians are feeling marginalized by American secularism, many immigrants, especially from Latin America, are bringing their vibrant faith to our churches. Joseph Castleberry, who spent twenty years on the mission field in Latin America, refers to these immigrants as "the new Pilgrims." As the first Pilgrims brought their vibrant faith to the New World, so the new Pilgrims are bringing their own faith to an America that is declining in religious vitality.[2]

Seventy-five percent of those who migrate to America profess to be Christians when they come to this country. That's five percent higher than the number of American residents who claim to be Christians. And the faith of these immigrants reveals an amazing intensity and sincerity that will compound their effect on America's faith.[3]

The Problems with Immigration

Working against the perceived immigration advantages are several growing and unsolved problems with both legal and illegal immigration.

Problems with Legal Immigration

Employment: American workers have lost jobs to immigrants who are willing to work for lower wages. And many have dropped out of the labor force altogether. The U.S. Department of Labor suggests that cheap immigrant labor is a substantial cause of the lack of growth in wages. Immigration also hurts the countries from which people emigrate as well-educated and highly skilled workers seek out better-paying jobs in America. Many students come to the U.S. for education and never return home.

Another growing problem is the failure of some ethnic groups to integrate into American life. Immigrants used to assimilate into the American "melting pot." Yes, America slowly changed over time with that assimilation. But today many ethnic groups refuse to assimilate and expect America to change to accommodate their preferences. An example is public schools in some southwestern border states where the Mexican flag is flown along with the American flag.

Lack of learning English is another flashpoint—some immigrants refuse to learn English. Their children grow up unable to find well-paying jobs due to lack of English language skills. Adherence to religious customs can also be a problem as illustrated by many Muslim communities of immigrants. Some American Muslim communities function more and more autonomously, setting up their own community standards and laws.

Because radical Islamic groups like the Muslim Brotherhood encourage and support these walled-off communities, they can become breeding grounds for anti-American and terroristic sentiments.

Many Americans are afraid that what has happened in Europe will happen in America. An open-arm policy to Muslim immigrants has resulted in an increase in radical Islamic terrorism in France, Germany, and England. Nearly all acts of terrorism in America have been committed by radicalized Muslims.

Problems with Illegal Immigration

According to three U.S. government agencies, illegal immigrants to America commit an extremely high number of crimes. More than 55,000 illegal aliens are imprisoned in the U.S. They have been arrested 459,614 times—an average of eight arrests per person. The crimes they have committed run the gamut: violent crimes, sex crimes, drug crimes, vehicle crimes, and more.[4]

The cost for social, educational, medical, and government services to illegal immigrants is staggering. By law, hospital emergency rooms cannot turn anyone away, and so many immigrants go there for medical services even when they are not emergencies. This results in crowded facilities that prevent true emergencies from being addressed. America's second-largest maternity-service hospital recently delivered 16,000 babies in one year, seventy percent of which were to illegal immigrant mothers in the first three months of that year. The cost? $70.7 million. The hospital subsequently had to add Spanish-speaking staff. And the University of Texas Southwestern Medical School now includes Spanish language requirements in its curriculum.[5]

The cost of social services for illegal immigrants is tens of billions of dollars annually. The drain on resources has put an unsustainable burden on the budgets of many smaller communities.

Perhaps the biggest problem facing America is that illegal immigration is just that: illegal. Our government has failed for years to address illegal immigration and now the problem is of crisis proportions. We have laws that are not being enforced, which creates an anarchist mentality in the society. Voting rights have long-term consequences. When illegal immigrants are allowed to vote they will vote for candidates and parties that will continue to provide free benefits and lax regulations. Who would vote for a political candidate who promises to make one's life harder?

These problems cause many to worry about America's future—and rightfully so.

The Past of Immigration

God's plan for one human family speaking one human language was thwarted by sin. Humanity was divided into groups as seen in the story of the Tower of Babel. The pride of the people to assume control over their own destiny caused God to confuse their languages. While that judgment stopped their prideful tower-building, it resulted in the birth of ethnic groups that populated the world (Genesis 11:1–9).

Dividing humanity into nations (Acts 17:26–27) has made it harder for humans to unite in powerful rebellion against God, creating a fractured human race. That is the price of sinful human pride and lust for power in the face of God. Modern one-world-government movements are not the will of God. Such a movement will characterize the sinful end times under the rule of the Antichrist.

So how are Christians to respond to those who show up at our borders or cross our borders illegally?

The Principles of Immigration

In Scripture we find principles for addressing the question of foreigners living in our midst or seeking refuge.

God's People Are to Assist the Stranger

God's admonition to Israel to care for strangers and sojourners was based not just on compassion but on their own history as "strangers in the land of Egypt" (Exodus 23:9). Travel in ancient times was treacherous; hospitality could mean the difference between life and death. Jeremiah exhorted King Zedekiah to "do no wrong and do no violence to the stranger, the fatherless, or the widow" (Jeremiah 22:3). The prophets were not kind to those who oppressed strangers in their midst (Ezekiel 22:29; Zechariah 7:10; Malachi 3:5).

God's People Are to Accept the Stranger

The Old Testament notes many non-Israelites who were accepted within Israel: Rahab a Canaanite (Joshua 6:25) and Ruth a Moabite (the book of

Ruth) are good examples. Both were honored in Israel and both were ancestors of Jesus Christ (Matthew 1:5-6). Uriah the Hittite (2 Samuel 11:1-17) and Ittai the Gittite (2 Samuel 15:19-22) were both soldiers loyal to King David. Doeg the Edomite was King Saul's chief herdsman (1 Samuel 21:7).

Jesus was accepting and welcoming of non-Israelites like the Samaritan woman (John 4:1-26) and a Canaanite woman (Matthew 15:21-28). And He made a Samaritan man the hero in a story He told about compassion (Luke 10:25-37). And Peter made it clear that "God shows no partiality" (Acts 10:34-35), a stance later affirmed by the apostle Paul (Galatians 3:28).

God's People Are to Assimilate the Stranger

Reading those examples, it is evident that in ancient Israel strangers (non-Israelites) who wanted to live in Israel were to be assimilated. They were subject to the same laws as were the native Israelites (Leviticus 18:26). Strangers (immigrants) were not free to live as they pleased. This seems harsh, but it was to keep at bay pagan customs and beliefs that could weaken Israel's faith and relationship with God over time. Strangers were subject to capital punishment just as Israelites were (Leviticus 24:16; Numbers 15:30).

Immigrants to Israel were expected to work and make their own way. When it came time to build the temple in Jerusalem, Solomon put 153,600 aliens to work as construction workers (2 Chronicles 2:17).

The principle was clear: If aliens would accept the culture and contribute to the national economy, they were welcomed. If they were unwilling to assimilate, they would be unwelcome.

The Perfection of Immigration

The ultimate goal of God's plan is to reunite humanity, restoring the unity planned in the beginning. Revelation 7:9-10 pictures a throng "from every nation, tribe, people and language" (NIV) worshiping God in heaven. Though we do not see that unity among nations and people today, we will in eternity. Peter referred to it as the "restoration of all things" (Acts 3:21). Even the prophets foresaw unity among humanity: Egyptians, Assyrians, Israelites together, "a blessing in the midst of the land" (Isaiah 19:24). The idea of peace between Israel and her Arab neighbors seems like a dream today, but the day will come when the temple of God "shall be called a house of prayer for all nations" (Isaiah 56:7). "In those days ten men from every language of the nations shall grasp the sleeve of a Jewish man, saying, 'Let us go with you, for we have heard that God is with you'" (Zechariah 8:23).

Christ's millennial kingdom will represent a time of peace and unity among all men due to the righteous reign of Christ as King. Every person is created in the image of God and is of great value to Him. That value will be recognized and celebrated.

We don't have that now, but we are enjoined to love others today with the same love God has always shown us (1 John 4:11). Therefore, we must treat strangers and foreigners among us as image-bearers of God, people whom He loves. The challenge is to know how to express that love in the midst of an unsolved problem like immigration and border security.

The problem centers on civil law. Scripture says we are to obey civil law because it is instituted by God for purposes of order and the safety of citizens (Romans 13:1–7; 1 Peter 2:13–14). America has immigration laws that our own government has failed to enforce. The result is millions of undocumented immigrants living among us.

A group of evangelical Christian leaders gathered in 2012 and produced a statement calling for immigration reform consistent with biblical principles. It contained well-thought-out recommendations, but of course the group had no power of enforcement. They could only add a biblical voice to the national discussion.

Rightly or wrongly, we have foreigners and strangers living among us. It is as if the mission field has come to America! James Kessler, in the weekly magazine of the Assemblies of God Church, asked this question: "How should Christians respond to the overwhelming tide of immigration—the influx of foreign, anti-Christian cultures and religions?" He answered his question by saying, "It is imperative that we take a new, long look at Christ's command and develop a responsible attitude toward Home Missions. America has become a mission field in the truest sense."[6]

As of this writing, the church I pastor in El Cajon, California, sponsors five international congregations: Arabic, Filipino, Iranian, Iraqi, and Hispanic. Our city is home to the largest population of Iraqi immigrants in the U.S.—approximately 25,000. Each of these five groups has worship services in their own language ranging in size from thirty to 700. We were recently given a church property in Encinitas, California, where we transmit by satellite English services in the morning and Spanish services in the afternoon. These two services reach around 900 Hispanics each week. Because our Hispanic pastor is such an excellent communicator, the two Hispanic TV stations in our area have given us two hours of free airtime to broadcast the Hispanic services. Almost every week in our main church service we hear testimonies of believers who are baptized—and often a translator is needed!

The point is, while our government sorts out the "immigration crisis" from a legal and practical standpoint, we can minister to the strangers and foreigners who are in our midst. In a Providential way, God has allowed millions of people to come to our country, many of whom have never been exposed to the Gospel of Christ at all. And we can tell them! We can show them how much God loves them by demonstrating that we love them.

Samuel Rodriguez has summarized the issue well:

> Immigration reform is both a vertical and horizontal issue. Vertically, the heart of God stands moved by the plight of immigrants and their suffering. Horizontally, passing immigration reform will serve as a reconciliatory prescription for a nation divided by partisan politics. Accordingly, it is the cross that prompts us to lift our hands toward heaven and to stretch our hands toward our neighbor. . . .
> It is the cross that compels us to declare that a human being cannot be illegal. It is the cross that drives us to reconcile the rule of law (Rom 13) with treating the immigrant as one of our own (Lev. 19).[7]

There is no better way to bring heaven to earth than to reach out to the strangers and foreigners among us and share the love of Christ.

APPLICATION

I. After the Flood, what was the eventual state of mankind (Genesis 11:6a)?

a. What was God's means of judgment that resulted in groups and eventually nations (Genesis 11:7–9)?

b. What particular act of emigration changed the course of world history? Where did this family travel "from" and "to" (Genesis 11:31; 12:1)?

c. What did the writer to the Hebrews call these early migrants (Hebrews 11:13)?

d. What is the chief motivation for migrants? What are they seeking (Hebrews 11:14, 16)?

e. What is the better country all believers are seeking?

2. In times of geo-political turmoil, on what can we rely (Acts 17:26)?

3. What command did Moses give to the people regarding strangers in their midst (Exodus 23:9)?

a. Why are immigrants often the most empathetic to other immigrants' plight?

b. What reason did the Israelites have for treating strangers with kindness?

4. What did the people of Israel do that drew the ire of the prophets?

   a. Ezekiel 22:29

      Zechariah 7:10

      Malachi 3:5

   b. With what groups of people within Israel did the prophets always mention the alien or stranger? What did all those people have in common?

5. Why was God so eager to allow aliens and strangers to find a home within Israel? What do Isaiah 42:6, 49:6, and 60:3 suggest is the reason?

   a. How brightly does the light of the Gospel shine in most countries compared to America?

   b. Why is that a reason for American Christians to welcome strangers and aliens?

6. Read Romans 13:1–7.

   a. What is the Christian's basic responsibility to government (verse 1a)?

   b. Why is that our responsibility (verse 1b)?

   c. How would you define the government's responsibility "for good" (verse 4) when it comes to immigration? What laws should the government enact?

   d. Is the current status of immigration in America "good"? How could it be made better?

7. What admonition concerning strangers is found in Hebrews 13:2?

DID YOU KNOW?

The same person is eventually both an immigrant and an emigrant depending on the perspective. An immigrant is a person who *comes* to a foreign country to establish residency (think: i = immigrant = *into*). And an emigrant is a person who *leaves* his or her own country to settle in a foreign country (think: e = emigrant = *exit*). So every emigrant who leaves his country eventually becomes an immigrant when he settles in another country. A 2012 Gallup survey found that 640 million people in the world would, if they could, emigrate to a different country. The United States was the top choice of countries to emigrate to, Britain being second.[8]

Notes

1. "US Immigration History Statistics," accessed March 18, 2016, http://m.emmigration.info/us-immigration-history-statistics.htm.
2. Joseph Castleberry, Ed.D., *The New Pilgrims: How Immigrants Are Renewing America's Faith and Values* (TN: Worthy Publishers, 2015).
3. Ibid., 4.
4. Summarized from Jim Kouri, "Illegal aliens linked to rise in crime statistics," *Renew America*, June 22, 2006, http://www.renewamerica.com/columns/kouri/ 060622. Based on statistics from the Government Accounting Office, U.S. Department of Justice, and National Security Institute. Accessed March 21, 2016.
5. Summarized from a circulating email confirmed by Snopes.com, August 2015, http://www.snopes.com/politics/immigration/parkland.asp. Accessed March 16, 2016.
6. James Kessler, "New Dimensions in Mission America," *Pentecostal Evangel*, August 4, 1985, 26.
7. Samuel Rodriquez, *Christians at the Border: Immigration, the Church, and the Bible* (Grand Rapids: Brazos Press, 2013), foreword.
8. Jon Clifton, "150 Million Adults Worldwide Would Migrate to the U.S.," Gallup, http://www.gallup.com/poll/153992/150-Million-Adults-Worldwide-Migrate.aspx. Accessed May 14, 2016.

LESSON 3

The Increase of Intolerance

In this lesson we consider the growing trend toward persecution of Christians in America and how to prepare for it.

OUTLINE

When we speak of persecution, most Christians think of physical torture or punishment. But that is too narrow. Persecution encompasses all manner of oppression against a person's faith commitments. In that sense, the persecution of Christians in America has already begun.

I. **The Substance of Christian Persecution**

II. **The Stages of Christian Persecution**
   A. Stage One: Stereotyping
   B. Stage Two: Marginalizing
   C. Stage Three: Threatening
   D. Stage Four: Intimidating
   E. Stage Five: Litigating

III. **The Story of Christian Persecution**
   A. Persecution of Christians in the Bible
   B. Persecution of Christians in History
   C. Persecution of Christians in Today's World

IV. The Side Effects of Christian Persecution
    A. Suffering Promotes Character
    B. Suffering Provokes Courage
    C. Suffering Proves Godliness
    D. Suffering Produces Joy
    E. Suffering Provides Rewards

V. The Strength to Face Christian Persecution
    A. Determine to Stand for Truth
    B. Draw Support from One Another
    C. Derive Your Security from the Lord

OVERVIEW

In the last few years, an increasing number of churches, businesses, and individuals have come under legal attack for standing on their biblical principles. These attacks have mostly been generated when Christians have resisted the decay of biblical sexual–moral standards in the U.S.

Jesus scolded the Pharisees for their inability to discern the signs of the times in their day (Matthew 16:3). The signs of *our* time could not be more clear: America is growing increasingly hostile toward biblical Christianity. The Bible is no longer America's moral compass. Those who hold to biblical principles are cited as intolerant at best and lawbreakers at worst.

The Substance of Christian Persecution

America's biblical foundation began to erode in the post-World War II prosperity which resulted in the protest culture of the 1960s. Freedom has been replaced by license. "If it feels good, do it" is now the guiding principle of American culture, pushing Christianity to the margins of the marketplace.

The Pew Research Center reports that Christianity is declining sharply in America. In 2014 about seventy percent of American adults identified as Christians.[1] But this figure is misleading. According to a study by sociologists C. Kirk Hadaway and Penny Long Marler published in *The Journal for the Scientific Study of Religion*, less than twenty percent of Americans regularly attend church on a weekly basis.[2] This statistic gives us a better indication of actual Christian commitment.

Dr. Paul Nyquist, the president of Moody Bible Institute in Chicago, writes, "Get ready. An exciting, yet terrifying era is beginning for American believers. As cultural changes sweep our country, we'll soon be challenged to live out what the Bible says about confronting and responding to persecution."[3]

The Stages of Christian Persecution

Five stages of religious suppression and persecution are taking place in America.

Stage One: Stereotyping

Today Christians are often stereotyped as ignorant, uneducated, backward, inhibited, homophobic, hateful, and intolerant. Movies and television portray Christians as the cultural "bad guy," the unreasonable character who is judgmental and out of step with the mainstream.

While it's true that some professing Christians do a poor job of representing the faith, these stereotypes do not reflect the reality of authentic Christianity. They grow out of the rising cultural prejudice against the Christian faith. Our duty is to live our convictions in a way that shows these slanderous pictures to be gross distortions of the truth.

Stage Two: Marginalizing

Many would prefer for Christianity not only to be criticized but to be marginalized—to be pushed so far to the periphery of society that it is, for all practical purposes, eliminated. If Christianity can't legally be eliminated, they want to force it behind closed doors. They want Christianity's influence on American culture to be removed. For example, the secularization of holidays like Christmas and Easter. And it's happening. Christian student organizations are now barred from many university campuses. Courts have eliminated Christmas carols in some public schools, and doctors and small business owners are being forced to serve homosexual clients.

Stage Three: Threatening

Many individuals have been fired from companies for expressing their religious beliefs and practices *on their own time*. The very thought that a practicing Christian might bring some harm or disrespect to a government agency or a company is driving these terminations. Or, more likely, it is the fear of a lawsuit by intolerant groups against agencies and companies. Companies figure it is easier to fire the Christian than to go through a lengthy adjudication of the employees' rights.

Stage Four: Intimidating

In 2001, California parents sued to prevent psychological testing on first, third, and fifth graders because the tests contained explicit sexual questions. They lost. The court's ruling: "Parents have no due process or privacy right to override the determinations of public schools as to the information to which their children will be exposed."[4] This is only one example. Similar cases of loss-of-rights now occur regularly and people are being forced into compliance by the government.

Stage Five: Litigating

Christian small business owners who have declined the business of homosexual patrons have been taken to court and fined. Some have lost their businesses and some have received death threats. Public schools have long been the target of activists like the ACLU. When they took steps to prevent any kind of religious expressions at the graduation ceremonies of a Florida high school, the students themselves struck back. They rose together and recited the Lord's Prayer on their own, motivating many in attendance to join them.[5]

Unless there is a great turnaround, we can expect lawsuits and court judgments to escalate against Christians who practice their faith. According to one writer, "Persecution could well accelerate to include Henry VIII-style seizure of church property and monies because of Christian leaders' refusal to bow to the doctrines of the State . . . even jail time for Christians is quite possible."[6]

Christians in America are not likely to experience the kinds of persecution and torture seen in other countries today. And yet, I never imagined a few decades ago that what is happening in America to Christians would be possible. So who knows what the future holds?

The Story of Christian Persecution

God's people have always been persecuted, even in the Old Testament (Hebrews 11:35–38). Christ was persecuted as were His apostles—as He warned them they would be (Matthew 10:16–20). To be persecuted for righteousness' sake means that we are hated or opposed solely for being a follower of Christ. When we are doing what is right and living for God, yet suffer because of it, that is persecution.

In America, we have traditionally held a too-narrow view of persecution—that it refers only to physical attacks. But persecution can include mental, spiritual, and emotional oppression brought about through any number of means, all for simply being a Christian. And *Christianity Today* magazine reminds us that "most persecution is not violence. Instead, it's a 'squeeze' of Christians in five spheres of life: private, family, community, national, and church."[7]

Why does the Christian message, and those who follow it, motivate such antagonism? Because it requires submission to God. Those antagonistic to the Gospel feel judged, and rightly so. Not judged by other Christians, but by God Himself. And without a proper understanding of God's *right* to judge sinners, that produces a backlash against God and His people. Ultimately, all are without excuse as Paul wrote in Romans 1:20–21. Because they don't like, and cannot silence, the message; opponents attack the messenger.

Persecution of Christians in the Bible

Persecution in the New Testament begins with Christ's birth in Bethlehem when Herod tried to kill Him when He was just a baby. Jesus was persecuted as an adult as was John the Baptist, the apostles, the deacon Stephen, the Christians living in Jerusalem, and the apostle Paul in extreme measure (2 Corinthians 11:22–29). All the apostles died grisly deaths at the hands of Christ's opponents.

It is amazing that the early Christians in Jerusalem, in the midst of persecution, bound themselves to one another and to the Lord and continued on. They pooled their resources and took care of each other (Acts 4:32–35). In fact, they even rejoiced that their persecution provided a great opportunity for God to display Himself (Acts 4:29–30).

Persecution of Christians in History

The Roman emperor Nero impaled Christians on stakes and set them afire as torches. He sent them into the arenas to be eaten by wild animals and killed by gladiators. He executed both Peter and Paul. Emperor Domitian declared himself to be "God the Lord" and demanded Christians worship him. When they refused, they were killed. The apostle John was exiled to Patmos by Domitian. Until Constantine became emperor and declared Christianity legal in AD 313, Christians were persecuted in the Roman Empire.

Millions more Christians have been killed in various parts of the world since the first century for various reasons. Stories abound of Christians willingly suffering persecution for the sake of their Savior. Catholic Queen Mary of England—called "Bloody Mary" for her execution of more than 300 Protestants—sentenced Henry VIII's former chaplain, Nicholas Ridley, to be burned. "As he was being tied to the stake, Ridley prayed, 'Oh, heavenly Father, I give unto thee most hearty thanks that thou hast called me to be a professor of thee, even unto death.'"[8]

Persecution of Christians in Today's World

Worldwide each month, 322 Christians are killed for their faith, 214 church buildings and Christian properties are destroyed, and 772 forms of violence are committed against individual Christians or Christian groups. Those figures add up to more than 15,000 incidents of serious persecution of Christians per year. This does not include the more than 200 million Christians who, according to the World Evangelical Alliance, are presently denied fundamental human rights just because of their faith. The top ten persecuting countries are North Korea, Iraq, Eritrea, Afghanistan, Syria, Pakistan, Somalia, Sudan, Iran, and Libya.[9] America could soon join this list.

The Side Effects of Christian Persecution

Let me suggest five ways persecution can be a positive thing for a Christian.

Suffering Promotes Character

The New Testament clearly teaches that tribulation—and that would include persecution—builds character: Romans 5:2–5; James 1:2–4. If you want proven character, persecution is one way to get it.

Suffering Provokes Courage

Courage is a reflection of the life of Christ in the Christian. Jesus was not a coward. He entrusted Himself to the Father and drank from the bitter cup of persecution. Peter and John told the Jewish officials that they would not stop preaching the Gospel, that it was their duty to obey God rather than man (Acts 4:19–20; 5:29). The apostle Paul's post-conversion life was a living display of courage (Philippians 1:20–21).

Suffering Proves Godliness

Paul wrote that all who want to live a godly life for Christ will suffer persecution (2 Timothy 3:12). Professing Christians who are not suffering may need to examine the depth of their godliness. Suffering is a form of cleansing and maturing (Hebrews 12:6; Peter 5:10). Jesus learned obedience through the things He suffered (Hebrews 5:8) and so can we. *Suffering* for Christ is a sure sign we are *living* for Christ (Romans 8:16–17).

Suffering Produces Joy

When Paul and Silas were confined to jail in Philippi, they contented themselves with "praying and singing hymns to God" (Acts 16:22–25). Peter and John went away from their persecution "rejoicing" at the privilege of suffering for Christ (Acts 5:41).

Suffering Provides Rewards

What are some of the rewards promised to those who endure persecution?

- Those who endure will be avenged (Revelation 6:9–11; 16:5–7; 18:20; 19:2).
- They will be rewarded with white robes, signifying holiness and purity (Revelation 6:11).
- They will be given perfect and abundant lives free of sorrow (Revelation 7:14–17).
- Heaven will rejoice over them because they did not shrink from death (Revelation 12:11–12).
- They will find eternal rest (Revelation 14:13).
- They will reign with Christ for 1,000 years (Revelation 20:4, 6).
- They will receive the crown of eternal life (James 1:12).
- They will have no more death to fear (1 Corinthians 15:54; Revelation 20:14).

The Strength to Face Christian Persecution

The time to prepare to face persecution is before it happens. If we wait until persecution arises, our emotions will rule the day. We must decide in the calm of commitment what we will do if persecution comes. The following are three things we can do to prepare.

Determine to Stand for Truth

In his famous Harvard commencement address, Aleksandr Solzhenitsyn said, "A decline in courage may be the most striking feature that an outside observer notices in the West in our days."[10] We as Christians must turn that criticism on its head. It is imperative that fear of rejection, criticism, or loss does not cower us into hiding our light. To live worthy of the Gospel is to stand for God's truth without bending. As Paul urged the Corinthians, "Watch, stand fast in the faith, be brave, be strong. Let all that you do be done with love" (1 Corinthians 16:13–14).

We must be prepared to take whatever criticism or persecution comes our way. We must be willing to be "fools for Christ's sake" (1 Corinthians 4:10). Paul gave us our rules of engagement: "Being reviled, we bless; being persecuted, we endure; being defamed, we entreat" (1 Corinthians 4:12–13). And we must be prepared to defend our faith (1 Peter 3:15–16).

Draw Support from One Another

Hebrews 10:24–25 says it best: "And let us consider one another in order to stir up love and good works, not forsaking the assembling of ourselves together, as *is* the manner of some, but exhorting one another, and so much the more as you see the Day approaching." When persecution comes, we need the support of the Body of Christ. We need the Church and the Church needs us. The worst place to be in the midst of persecution is alone. Elijah survived the persecution of Queen Jezebel by discovering there were 7,000 more in Israel who were standing firm against the wicked queen and king (1 Kings 19:14–18).

We too need the company of others like ourselves with whom we can share encouragement, struggles, and victories. In today's culture this need is greater than ever. Now in the minority and under attack, it's easy for us to feel alone and discouraged, as Elijah did. But in the company of fellow believers, we draw strength, discipline, knowledge, encouragement, support, and love from each other. A courageous example can spur any one of us to say, "If she can do it, by God's grace so can I."

Derive Your Security from the Lord

We must keep our eye on the prize when the pressure of persecution hits. We belong to Christ; we are on our way to heaven; nothing can separate us from the love of God in Christ; all things work together for the good of those who belong to Him. The greatest temptation in the face of persecution is to do *anything* to save our life. But remember Jesus' words: "For whoever desires to save his life will lose it, but whoever loses his life for My sake will find it" (Matthew 16:25).

According to C. S. Lewis we are in "enemy-occupied territory." There will be attacks, even some casualties. But our citizenship is in heaven. We are simply waiting here on earth for Him to appear from heaven to transform us into His own image (Philippians 3:20–21).

What will you do if repression and coercion in America ultimately lead to persecution? Don't wait until it happens to decide who you serve. Draw a line in the sand and stand on the side of Christ. Trust your past, present, and future to the One who has promised to save you forever.

APPLICATION

I. Read Hebrews 11:35–40.

   a. What is the overall context of this passage? (Remember: Hebrews 11 is the "Hall of Faith" chapter.)

   b. Why were some of these martyrs willing to die, refusing to be released from torture (verse 35)?

c. How does verse 36 suggest that personal ridicule qualifies as persecution? (See "mockings.") Have you suffered this kind of persecution for your faith?

d. How is being "tempted" a form of persecution (verse 37)? Would someone lay a trap hoping for your moral failure?

e. What is true even when a Christian dies from persecution (verses 39–40)?

f. Why is citizenship in heaven the ultimate hope for those who are persecuted (Philippians 3:20)? Who can take that away from you?

2. What was the first act of persecution recorded in the New Testament (Matthew 2:1–16)?

3. What happened to John the Baptist (Mark 6:25–29)?

4. How was Jesus treated during His short time on earth?

a. Luke 4:28–30

Luke 13:31

John 5:16–18

John 8:37–40

b. What did Jesus learn through His persecutions (Hebrews 5:8)?

c. Why is discomfort or suffering the only place where obedience can be learned?

5. Describe what happened to Peter and the apostles in Jerusalem after Christ's ascension:

a. Acts 4:1–3, 18

Acts 5:17–18

Acts 12:1–4

b. How did the apostles react to this persecution (Acts 4:19–20; 5:29)?

c. What did they ask God to do for them (Acts 4:29–30)? Given how the Jewish leaders would respond, what were they asking God for? (More

_____.)

d. What was the early church in Jerusalem forced to do (Acts 8:1)?

e. Explain what the early church father, Tertullian, meant: "The blood of the martyrs is the seed of the church."

6. Summarize the kinds of things the apostle Paul suffered for the Gospel (2 Corinthians 6:4–5; 11:22–29).

7. How would you describe your "persecution quotient"? How would you respond if persecution of Christians in America begins to affect your livelihood or your life?

DID YOU KNOW?

The most comprehensive account of Christian persecution was compiled by John Foxe in England and published in 1563. It is still in print today as *Foxe's Book of Martyrs*, its original title being too long: *Actes and Monuments of these Latter and Perillous Days, Touching Matters of the Church*. Written during the reign of Protestant Queen Elizabeth I, it was originally published in five books. It covered the earliest Christian persecutions, the Catholic Inquisitions in the medieval period, the early English Protestant movement, the separation of the Church of England from Rome, and finally the persecutions of Protestants by Catholic Queen Mary who herself was responsible for executing more than 300 Protestant leaders in England.

Notes

1. "America's Changing Religious Landscape," *Pew Research Center*, May 12, 2015, http://www. pewforum.org/2015/05/12/americas-changing-religious-landscape/. Accessed April 11, 2016.

2. Kelly Shattuck, "7 Startling Facts: An Up Close Look at Church Attendance in America," *Church Leader*, http://www.churchleaders.com/pastors/pastor-articles/ 139575-7-startling-facts-an-up-close-look-at-church-attendance-in-america.html. Accessed April 11, 2016.

3. J. Paul Nyquist, *Prepare* (Chicago: Moody Publishers, 2015), 10.

4. "Ninth Circuit Decision Denies Parents' Rights," *Education Reporter*, December 2005, http:// www.eagleforum.org/educate/2005/dec05/9th-circuit.html. Accessed April 6, 2016.

5. Bob Unruh, "Graduating Students Defy ACLU," *WND*, June 5, 2009, http://www.wnd. com/2009/06/100274/. Accessed April 7, 2016.

6. Fay Voshell, "Persecution of Christians in America: It's Not Just 'Over There,'" *American Thinker*, May 10, 2015, http://www.americanthinker.com/articles/2015/ 05/persecution_of_christians_in_america_its_not_just_over_there.html.

7. "Inside the Persecution Numbers," *Christianity Today*, March 2014, 14.

8. "Bishops Ridley and Latimer Burned," *Christianity.com,* http://www.christianity.com/church/ church-history/timeline/1501-1600/ bishops-ridley-and-latimer-burned-11629990.html. Accessed April 9, 2016.

9. "Christian Persecution," *Open Doors*, https://www.opendoorsusa.org/christian-persecution/. Accessed April 7, 2016.

10. Aleksandr Solzhenitsyn, *Harvard Commencement Address*, June 8, 1978.

LESSON 4

The Apathy of America

SELECTED SCRIPTURES

*In this lesson we survey America's past blessings,
present condition, and prospects for the future.*

OUTLINE

Amerika was founded by people steeped in biblical principles. The nation grew with a Christian consensus in government and the marketplace. But that is no longer true; America is a post-Christian nation. America's past blessings are unmistakable, but her future is anything but clear.

I. **America and the Providence of God**

II. **America and the Provision of God**
   A. The Blessing of Our Forefathers
   B. The Blessing of Our Freedom
   C. The Blessing of Our Fortunes

III. **America and the Plan of God**
   A. America May Be Included in the European Coalition
   B. America May Be Invaded by Outside Forces
   C. America May Be Infected with Moral Decay
   D. America May Be Incapacitated Because of the Rapture

IV. America and the People of God
    A. Our Living Hope Rests in the Power of the Resurrection
    B. Our Living Hope Rests in the Promise of Our Reward
    C. Our Living Hope Rests in Our Protection Until Christ's Return

OVERVIEW

Almost 200 years ago, Professor Alexander Tyler wrote the following words about the fall of the Athenian Republic more than 2,000 years earlier:

> A democracy cannot exist as a permanent form of government. It can only exist until the voters discover that they can vote themselves money from the public treasury. From that moment on, the majority always votes for the candidates promising the most money from the public treasury, with the result that a democracy always collapses over loose fiscal policy, always followed by dictatorship.
>
> The average age of the world's greatest civilizations has been 200 years. These nations have progressed through the following sequence: From bondage to spiritual faith, from spiritual faith to great courage, from courage to liberty, from liberty to abundance, from abundance to selfishness, from selfishness to complacency, from complacency to apathy, from apathy to dependency and from dependency back to bondage.[1]

An honest appraisal of our nation would seem to indicate that we are moving steadily toward the end of Professor Tyler's sequential list. It is not a stretch to describe our nation as "an apathetic nation." If Professor Tyler's analysis is correct, a return to dependency and bondage could be just around the corner for America, something Charles Ryrie warns has historical precedent:

> Nations rise and nations fall. It is a two-way street. The might of ancient Babylon lasted only 86 years. The powerful Persian Empire

did better—208 years. The glory of Greece was eclipsed after 268 years. Mighty Rome ruled for almost 9 centuries. The British Empire endured for about 250 years. The United States of America has celebrated her bicentennial. If we make it to a tri-centennial, we will beat the averages.[2]

To understand how devastating America's apathy is, it helps to go back to the beginning of the nation's story.

America and the Providence of God

The nation's first president, George Washington, was a man of humility. While he came from a prominent Virginia family, and was asked to command the Revolutionary War army and lead the Constitutional Convention, he reluctantly eschewed all royal titles when he was elected the first president, settling on "Mr. President."

After his inauguration on April 30, 1789, President Washington spoke to the assembled leaders of the nation. One senator observed that the president seemed nervous—more nervous than he ever was in the midst of battles with the British. I don't think stage fright was the problem. I'm confident the first president of America was overwhelmed by a sense of Providential responsibility. The Founding Fathers were thoroughly versed in Scripture. They knew that it is God who establishes rulers and nations, and removes them when needed. They knew verses like Job 12:23: "He makes nations great, and destroys them; He enlarges nations, and guides them." And Daniel 2:20–21: "He removes kings and raises up kings; He gives wisdom to the wise and knowledge to those who have understanding." And other passages like Deuteronomy 32:8; 1 Chronicles 29:11–12; Proverbs 21:1; Daniel 4:17, 34–35; Acts 17:24, 26.

Most of America's leaders no longer have any sense of Providential responsibility. "In God We Trust" is still on our money, and the president still says "God bless the United States of America," but that is the extent of how much God is allowed into the hallowed halls of government. And it is the same in the public square—God has been moved to the margins of society.

Example: In 2011, NBC covered the U.S. Open Golf Championship. Twice during the broadcast, a segment was featured with children reciting the Pledge of Allegiance to America. Both times, the words "under God" and "indivisible" were omitted. After significant pushback, NBC said it made a mistake. But they did the same thing in 2015 in a promo for an up-coming television show called, ironically, "Allegiance." A chorus of voices is heard reciting the Pledge of Allegiance and, again, omitting the words "under God."[3]

From the banning of prayer in schools to changing "Merry Christmas" to "Happy Holidays" to the removal of the Ten Commandments from statehouse buildings . . . America is a changing nation.

America and the Provision of God

In 1815, President James Madison proclaimed these words to our nation:

> No people ought to feel greater obligations to celebrate the good-ness of the Great Disposer of Events of the destiny of nations than the people of the United States . . . . And to the same Divine author of Every Good and Perfect Gift we are indebted for all those privileges and advantages, religious as well as civil, which are so richly enjoyed in this favored land.

The Blessing of Our Forefathers

The American democratic republic has long been hailed as the most bril-liant form of government ever implemented. What was the source of these brilliant, revolutionary ideas? The Judeo-Christian Scriptures. Moses gave Israel a written constitution; a tripartite government of prophets, priests, and kings ruled a decentralized (12 tribal states) nation; all were equal before the throne of God. The Founders didn't think America was Israel or the Kingdom of God, but they certainly recognized the wisdom of how God governs and applied it freely to America's system of governance. America's presidents throughout history, until recently, have been more than happy to acknowledge God's blessings on America.

The Blessing of Our Freedom

Why do more emigrants strive to come to America than to other coun-tries? For the chance to be free! Jesus expressed the yearning of the human spirit when He said "the truth shall make you free" (John 8:32). The Founders acknowledged as much when they noted the Creator's endowment of "unalienable Rights" such as "Life, Liberty, and the pursuit of Happiness."

The Founders wanted nothing to hinder the creatures' fulfillment of the Creator's blessing of freedom. They designed a government that would be *out of* the citizens' way, not *in* the citizens' way. Yet freedom comes with responsibilities and at a high cost. Think of all who have died in the last 250 years in defense of our freedom. Some are defending freedom on foreign shores at this very hour. If our children are to have the same freedoms we enjoy, we will have to defend them against all attacks.

If we begin to take our freedom for granted, it is a small step toward taking the Author of freedom for granted Himself. While our greatest freedom is the freedom from sin (John 8:36), God wants us to be free from tyranny as well. If we stop being willing to pay the price required to defend both, then apathy is at our door.

The Blessing of Our Fortunes
America has been the most prosperous nation in human history.

1. Financial Blessings
Wealth isn't always a sign of God's blessing, but it would have been for Israel (Deuteronomy 28:1–14; 1 Kings 10:1–9). And multiplication and prosperity are built into God's creation. Nature produces harvests of abundance as does the wise investor (Matthew 25:14–30). Profit and abundance speak of the greatness and generosity of God.

America has long been a nation of wealth whether measured by GDP or the number of billionaires. Perhaps America's wealth is tied to its generosity. What is important about wealth is not its quantity but what we do with it (1 Timothy 6:9–10; 17–19). And America has always been generous to less-fortunate countries, both nationally and individually.

How is America able to be generous? Because of the blessing of God. This was the conclusion of King David when he and his leaders gave generously to fund the building of the Temple in Jerusalem. Everything comes from God (1 Chronicles 29:14).

2. Intellectual Blessings

America's universities aren't the oldest but they are among the world's best. America's oldest universities were founded in New England for the training of ministers of the Gospel. Schools like Harvard, Yale, Princeton, Brown, Colgate, Columbia, and Dartmouth still have mottos that reflect their original biblical worldview and purpose. Sadly, all these universities have abandoned their Gospel-centered curricula and focus. But academically, American universities remain among the best in the world.

3. Military Blessings

There had been no attacks on American soil since the Revolutionary War until September 11, 2001. It's like a hedge of protection had surrounded our nation. Article Four, Section Four of the Constitution states that the federal government will protect the states against invasion. By God's grace that mandate has been carried out. America's military has played a key role in defending freedom and liberty around the world.

4. Religious Blessings

From its founding, America has been a Christian-consensus nation. But in the 1960s, the term "post-Christian" began to be applied to our nation. In spite of the large percentage of American's who declare themselves to be Christians, Christianity is no longer seen as the guiding worldview in government and the marketplace. Secularism is on the rise. It is another danger sign for America that she is becoming a secular, if not agnostic, nation. Christianity is declining while non-Christian faiths are increasing. Increasing most of all are the "unaffiliated."[4]

In spite of America's blessed beginning and history, the future is a question mark.

America and the Plan of God

By many measurements, America is still a great nation. But spiritually and morally, it's hard to make a case that America has not changed. The question must be asked, "If God is responsible for America's past blessings, and America turns her back on God, what does the future hold?" Many have asked, "Does the Bible say anything about America's future?" Many modern nations are mentioned in the Bible—those that have ancient foundations in the biblical world—but America is not one of them.

In my book, *What in the World Is Going On?*, I suggested four possible futures for America.

America May Be Included in the European Coalition

The coming Antichrist will lead a coalition of ten modern nations, likely centered in Europe. It is possible that America will have become so weak morally and spiritually that she joins this coalition as a means of economic survival as the Antichrist's power and authority increase. In this case, America will be judged by God along with the Antichrist at the end of the Tribulation.

America May Be Invaded by Outside Forces

Today, eight nations besides America possess nuclear capability, and not all are friendly toward the United States. It is possible that America could suffer nuclear, cyber, or other attacks that could cripple her economy beyond immediate repair. Such an attack could seriously damage the nation and cripple our standing in the world.

America May Be Infected with Moral Decay

If revival does not come to America, then we put ourselves at risk for judgment from God. The history of Israel shows that God does not wait forever for people to repent and return to Him. America is showing no signs of doing so at present and may never. Thirteen times in the period of the book of Judges, the cycle of rebellion, retribution, repentance, and restoration was repeated. America has seen revivals in the past and could again. If she does not, she will atrophy into judgment at worst and insignificance at best. The terror attack of 9/11 showed signs of bringing America to its senses. But those signs quickly subsided as America returned her focus to materialism and pleasure.

America May Be Incapacitated Because of the Rapture

When the Rapture occurs, a significant portion of America's "salt and light" will be removed from earth. Not only that, but the restraining power of the Holy Spirit will be removed (2 Thessalonians 2:5–12). When that happens, a downward spiral will be set in motion from which the nation would not likely recover. America would suffer the terrible Tribulation judgments outlined in Revelation. If none of the other three scenarios happen first, this one eventually will.

America and the People of God

America is a nation out of step with the will of God. The book of 1 Peter is one for the American Church. It was written to Christians who were trying to survive in a culture that was out of step with its Creator (1 Peter 5:6). The surrounding nations did not accept those Christians or understand them. Peter calls his readers "pilgrims"—they were exiles, strangers, and foreigners in their own lands (1 Peter 2:11). All Christians are spiritual foreigners just passing through this world, so Peter's letter is one we should be very familiar with. He reminds his readers that our hope is not in earthly resources, but in God alone.

Our Living Hope Rests in the Power of the Resurrection (1 Peter 1:3)

God has "begotten us again to a living hope through the resurrection of Jesus Christ from the dead." We have hope because Christ conquered death and the grave. Even if the worst should come to America and we lose our physical life in some way, we still have hope because of the resurrection. Because Christ lives, we live! Our hope and our future do not depend on the status of our nation. We want it to be peaceful and stable so the Gospel can be spread (1 Timothy 2:1–4). But our hope is in our future resurrection, not in political stability.

Our Living Hope Rests in the Promise of Our Reward (1 Peter 1:4)

There is an "inheritance incorruptible and undefiled and that does not fade away, reserved in heaven for you," Peter writes.

1. An Untarnished Inheritance

People in Peter's day lived in fear of the Roman army coming in and "spoiling" (corrupting) their land and property. But our reward in heaven is completely off-limits; it is un-spoilable.

2. An Undefiled Inheritance

Our inheritance is unstained; holy, pure, and clean (Revelation 21:27).

3. An Unfading Inheritance

The glory of America and other nations may fade away, but our inheritance is permanent and eternal (Matthew 6:19–20).

4. An Uncontested Inheritance

Our inheritance is reserved, guaranteed by God Himself. The Holy Spirit is the seal of that guarantee (Ephesians 1:14).

Our Living Hope Rests in Our Protection Until Christ's Return (1 Peter 1:5)

We are "kept by the power of God through faith for salvation ready to be revealed in the last time." Verse 4 says our inheritance is reserved for us and verse 5 says we are reserved for our inheritance. We can only win!

While we wait to receive our inheritance there are four things we must do:

- Pay our taxes (Matthew 17:24–27)
- Pray for our leaders (1 Timothy 2:1–3)
- Participate in the process (1 Peter 4:13)
- Persevere in the race (Hebrews 10:36)

In Jesus Christ we have a sure and certain hope for the future. We pray for our nation while we praise God for our citizenship in heaven.

APPLICATION

I. Read Job 12:23–25.

   a. What four things does Job say God does relative to nations (verse 23)?

   b. What do verses 24–25 say about how God directs the actions of world leaders ("chiefs")?

c. What is the general context of these verses? What is Job saying about God (verses 13–22)?

d. How do these verses provide confidence when we survey the chaotic geo-political landscape of the world?

2. When America elects a president every four years, who is really in charge (Daniel 2:21)?

3. If God is "head over all" (1 Chronicles 29:11), how does that give us comfort about the future?

4. What can God do in the heart of any "king" (Proverbs 21:1)?

   a. Why doesn't God change a leader's heart to prevent him from doing bad things? (Think about what God allowed the kings of Assyria and Babylon to do to Israel, or the Pharaohs of Egypt.)

   b. Why must we trust that even the evil actions of "kings" are part of God's plan?

5. How did God's sovereign actions cause the pagan king of Babylon to respond (Daniel 4:17, 34–35)?

6. Summarize the blessings that were promised to Israel if she obeyed God's covenant (Deuteronomy 28:1–14).

    a. In general, what would happen if Israel disobeyed God's covenant (Deuteronomy 28:15–68)?

    b. How does Deuteronomy 28:12b suggest whether America is in a state of blessing or cursing?

7. Read 1 Chronicles 29:14–17a.

    a. What is the source of any nation's wealth (verse 14)?

    b. What does verse 15 suggest about what man possesses by himself? How wealthy are "aliens and pilgrims" normally? What hope do they have?

    c. How does verse 16 illustrate the principle of using wealth for God's glory?

    d. What does verse 17 suggest about wealth being a test? What is God testing?

e. What does America's financial situation suggest about how we have fared in this test?

8. What guarantee do we have from God that our future is not dependent on what happens to America (Ephesians 1:13–14)?

9. What spiritual responsibility do we have relative to our political leaders (1 Timothy 2:1–2)?

DID YOU KNOW?

After George Washington's inauguration in New York City, he and members of Congress worshipped at St. Paul's Chapel in what is today lower Manhattan. It is just steps from Ground Zero where the former World Trade Center towers collapsed. Miraculously, the chapel was not destroyed; not even a window pane was broken. On that day, George Washington said in his speech to Congress, "Since we ought to be no less persuaded that the propitious smiles of Heaven, can never be expected on a nation that disregards the eternal rules of order and right, which Heaven itself has ordained." The fall of two towers dedicated to American commerce stand in stark contrast to the preservation of the chapel where the first President worshiped after warning Congress about disregarding God's "rules of order and right."

Notes

1. Commonly attributed to Alexander Tyler, a Scottish lord and history professor in the University of Edinburgh in the late eighteenth century, http://theroadtoemmaus.org/RdLb/21PbAr/Hst/US/DmocAthnsUS.htm.
2. Charles Ryrie, *The Best Is Yet to Come* (Chicago: Moody Press, 1981), 106.
3. "Coats Asks NBC for Explanation of Why 'Under God' Omitted from Pledge during U.S. Open Broadcast," Website of U.S. Senator Dan Coats, June 21, 2011, https://www.coats.senate.gov/newsroom/press/release/coats-asks-nbc-for-explanation-of-why-under-god-omitted-from-pledge-during-us-open-broadcast. Accessed May 3, 2016). Also Todd Starnes, "NBC omits 'God' from Pledge of Allegiance . . . again," Fox News Opinion website, January 8, 2015, http://www.foxnews.com/opinion/2015/01/08/nbc-omits-god-from-pledge-allegiance-again.html. Accessed May 3, 2016.
4. "America's Changing Religious Landscape," *Pew Research Center*, May 12, 2015, http://www.pewforum.org/2015/05/12/americas-changing-religious-landscape/. Accessed May 4, 2016.

LESSON 5

The Remedy of Revival

2 CHRONICLES 34-36

In this lesson we learn about the history of American revivals and what it takes to bring revival again.

OUTLINE

From the Old Testament to the present day, revivals have come when apathy and sin have dominated. But we don't have to be apathetic about revival, waiting for it to "happen." Revivals happen one person at a time, and they can begin with a single committed soul.

I. Revival in the Bible
   A. A Humble Leader
   B. A Holy Book
   C. A Hungry People

II. Revival in America
   A. The Great Awakening: The 1740s
   B. The Second Great Awakening: The Early 1800s
   C. The Third Great Awakening: The 1850–60s

D. The Global Revival: The Early 1900s

E. The Jesus Movement: The 1960–70s

III. A Two-Fold Plan for Revival

A. Pray for Revival Personally

B. Practice Revival Personally

OVERVIEW

We often encounter the word "revival" in the news. The economy needs revival, an older Broadway show is experiencing a revival, and a run-down part of town is experiencing a revival with new housing and shopping. And it's also used of athletes who have been through a slump in their careers, then suddenly experience a revival of performance and interest by the media.

One such athlete is the pro-basketball player, Jeremy Lin, who is one of the first Asian-American players in the NBA. He was a walk-on at Harvard and, in his senior year, led the Crimson to a winning season. But the pro teams weren't interested. Finally, the New York Knicks gave him a contract, and he took Manhattan by storm. But then he battled injuries and surgeries and his career waned. In 2015, he began playing for the Charlotte Hornets and experienced a revival in his career.

Lin is happy for his basketball revival, but there is another revival he is more concerned about: a revival in the worldwide body of Christ. As a committed Christian, Jeremy Lin is praying that God will send genuine spiritual and moral revival to the Church.

I couldn't agree more with this standout athlete! America is in desperate need of spiritual and moral revival. That is the subject of this lesson. May we join with the psalmist who wrote, "Will You not revive us again, that Your people may rejoice in You?" (Psalm 85:6)

Revival in the Bible

Second Chronicles is the Bible's handbook on revival. Chapter 34 describes the remnant that returned from Babylon to rebuild Jerusalem and the temple and keep hope alive in Israel. But it would take a revival among the people.

Second Chronicles 34–35 describes a major revival under King Josiah. The evil King Manasseh had ruled Judah for 55 years, allowing the nation to sink to terrible depths of depravity. When Manasseh died his likewise evil son, Amon, took the throne for two years. Then came King Josiah—grandson of Manasseh, son of Amon—to the throne at age eight. By the grace of God, Josiah had a heart for righteousness (2 Chronicles 34:2).

A Humble Leader

In the eighth year of his reign, at age 16, Josiah "began to seek the God of his father David." And at age twenty he began purging Judah and Jerusalem of idols and high places of idol worship (2 Chronicles 34:3). At age 26 Josiah began a huge project to restore the temple in Jerusalem to its former glory (verses 10–12).

A Holy Book

During the temple renovations, the workers found a long-lost copy of the Book of the Law and brought it to Josiah (verse 14–17). Josiah was shocked when he read the words of God's covenant and saw how far the nation had fallen. He called for a prophet to come and help him understand the will of God. Huldah the prophet assured Josiah that because of his humility before God, the nation would receive help (verse 27–28).

A Hungry People

Encouraged by Huldah's words, Josiah announced a revival meeting, and everyone gathered at the temple. Josiah read the words of the Book of the Covenant to the people and committed himself and the nation to keeping God's statutes (verses 30–31). The people followed the king's lead and committed themselves to reviving the nation, including the reinstitution of Passover (2 Chronicles 35:18–19). The nation followed the Lord for "all [Josiah's] days" (2 Chronicles 34:33).

Josiah led the revival from the throne, and Jeremiah the prophet led from the pulpit. The prophets Zephaniah and Nahum joined in. I believe Josiah's revival was responsible for the shaping of Daniel and his three friends who were later taken to Babylon.

Future generations always feel the impact of revival. That is certainly true for the revivals that have occurred in America.

Revival in America

Past revivals prove an important point: Revivals are possible! That is good news for us in our day. Following is a survey of five periods of revival in America that impacted the nation and the world.

The Great Awakening: The 1740s

This awakening is one of the most famous movements in the history of American Christianity. The Pilgrims who landed on America's East Coast in 1620 arrived with Bibles in hand. Their intent was to gain religious freedom. The Puritans followed the Pilgrims and began founding colleges for the training of ministers and students from a biblical perspective—colleges like Harvard and Yale.

But the spiritual fervor of the colonies began declining in the 1600s. Godly preachers began to bemoan the spiritual condition of the people and churches. In the 1720s God unleashed a revival in the Colonies. It began in New England and spread to other states, mainly through the efforts of young people.

The name most associated with the Great Awakening is Jonathan Edwards, a pastor in Northampton, Massachusetts. Edwards was a prodigy, a genius. He entered Yale at age twelve and graduated when he was barely fifteen years old. He was ordained at age nineteen, was teaching at Yale at age twenty, and later became president of Princeton. His sermon, "Sinners in the Hands of an Angry God" is the most famous sermon in American history.

He preached that sermon on Sunday, July 8, 1741, and great repentance broke out in the service. The fear of hell spread throughout the village with people begging God for mercy and salvation. Five hundred people were converted that night, sparking a revival that would see thousands enter the kingdom.

British evangelists like John Wesley and George Whitefield were preaching in England and in America, seeing similar results as happened with Edwards. Converts filled the colonies; new theological training schools were opened: Princeton, Rutgers, Dartmouth, and Brown. Missionaries went into the wooded frontiers to evangelize Native Americans. This revival set the stage for the American Revolution.

The Second Great Awakening: The Early 1800s

After the Revolutionary War, Christianity in America spiraled into another decline. Efforts toward advancing the kingdom of God were eclipsed by efforts to build a new nation. Rationalism from the European Enlightenment began infiltrating universities and politics. People flooded into the frontier, west of the Appalachian Mountains, where few churches existed. Even in towns and cities, only a small percentage of the people attended church. Intellectuals like Voltaire in France, and his disciple in America, Thomas Paine, attacked Christianity. Most professors at the universities were no longer professing Christians. The same could be said for most students.

The great historian J. Edwin Orr has written that "the last two decades of the eighteenth century were the darkest period, spiritually and morally, in the history of American Christianity."[1]

Thankfully, revival came again. It started at Hampden-Sydney College in Virginia. The president of the college joined a small group of students in praying for revival and God answered. More than half the students repented and believed. The revival spread to other colleges and onto the American frontier. Outdoor revival meetings in Kentucky in 1801 clogged the roads as thousands upon thousands came to places like Cane Ridge to repent. Multiple preachers preached at the same time to different portions of the huge crowds. People sang, shouted, fell to the ground weeping, and were gloriously converted.

Preachers spread out from these meetings to all parts of the frontier and the East Coast. In 1806, students praying at Williams College in Massachusetts committed to go anywhere in the world God might send them. In 1812, Adoniram and Ann Judson sailed from Salem, Massachusetts, as America's first foreign missionaries. Thousands of churches began sending missionaries which led to the modern missionary movement—a result of the Second Great Awakening.

Other results came: the abolition movement, prison reform, child labor laws, women's rights, and rescue missions. Untold numbers of parachurch mission organizations sprang up, many of which are well-known today.

The Third Great Awakening: The 1850–60s

The pendulum swung back toward apathy by the middle of the nineteenth century. In 1858, another revival broke out. It began with a small prayer meeting in a Dutch Reformed Church in New York City. Within a few months, 50,000 people in the city were meeting for prayer. The movement spread to other major cities. Estimates are that between one and two million souls were saved.

At the height of the revival, offices and stores across the nation closed for prayer at noon. Newspapers and telegraph offices were flooded with news of the prayer meetings. From this revival, the YMCA was birthed in America along with Moody Bible Institute and several youth movements. When the Civil War broke out, tens of thousands of soldiers on both sides attended prayer and preaching services and were saved.

Gospel preaching and singing flourished during the Third Great Awakening. Our hymnbooks today still contain the hymns of Ira Sankey, Fanny Crosby, and others who penned songs of worship and revival: "Revive Us Again" and "Blessed Assurance" being examples.

The Global Revival: The Early 1900s

After the Civil War, the light of revival dimmed again. As after the Revolutionary War, recovering from the Civil War occupied the energy of the nation. But in the beginning of the twentieth century, a revival broke out (possibly) in Wales in the United Kingdom.

When a young Bible student named Evan Roberts preached a sermon in his village of Loughor, seventeen people attended to hear his four points: confess sin, put away doubtful habits, obey the Holy Spirit, and confess Christ openly. But by the end of the week there were sixty converts and a revival was under way. Within three months, 100,000 people were added to church rolls in Wales.

Roberts went to Liverpool in England and continued to preach. People from England, Ireland, Scotland, Europe, and America streamed to Liverpool to hear him. Thousands believed. The revival spread to all those countries and more including South Africa, India, Korea, China, Japan, Brazil, Indonesia, and more.

Cities and colleges in America were again turning to God and His Word. The revival reached the West Coast among students at Seattle

Pacific College in 1905. Portland, Oregon, experienced such a move of the Spirit that it is still called "Portland's Pentecost."[2] The Azusa Street Revival in Los Angeles in 1906 kicked off the Pentecostal movement. Itinerant preachers found their way into the Appalachian Mountains and started churches, many of which still stand today.

There has not been another global movement like that of 1905–1910, although the post-World War II years saw the birth of organizations that developed worldwide ministries: Campus Crusade for Christ (now Cru), Youth for Christ, the Billy Graham Evangelistic Association, and others.

The Jesus Movement: The 1960–70s

Then came "the Sixties"—the most turbulent cultural decade in American history. President Kennedy and his brother, Bobby, and Martin Luther King, Jr. were all assassinated. The Vietnam War divided the country as did racial tensions. There were riots on campuses and in the streets. Drugs and rock music dominated young peoples' lives. Watergate brought government to a standstill in the early '70s. President Nixon resigned in shame.

In 1967, a Christian couple opened a coffee house in the Haight-Ashbury district of San Francisco, ground zero for sex, drugs, and rock and roll. Other Christian coffee houses began opening up and down the West Coast. Long-haired hippies found Jesus and waded into the Pacific Ocean to be baptized. A revival called "The Jesus Movement" was born.

Billy Graham wrote a book called *The Jesus Generation*. *Look* and *Time* magazines wrote cover stories about "the Jesus People." Pastor Chuck Smith started Calvary Chapel, a church that welcomed this new generation of believers. They brought their guitars, formed bands, wrote songs, and birthed a new wave of worship music. Explo '72 drew 80,000 young people to the Cotton Bowl in Dallas for a week. Colleges experienced revival. Many of today's church leaders came to Christ during "the Jesus Movement." Thousands of college students were discipled by Campus Crusade, the Navigators, InterVarsity Christian Fellowship, and other campus ministries. Many of those students joined the staffs of those organizations, multiplying their impact.

We need another revival today. In his book, *The Secret of Christian Joy*, Vance Havner writes:

The greatest need of America is an old-fashioned, heaven-born, God-sent revival. Throughout the history of the Church, when clouds have hung lowest, when sin has seemed blackest and faith has been weakest, there have always been a faithful few who have not sold out to the devil nor bowed the knee to Baal, who have feared the Lord and thought upon His Name and have not forsaken the assembling of themselves together. These have besought the Lord to revive His work in the midst of the years, and in the midst of the fears and tears, and in wrath to remember mercy. God has always answered such supplication, filling each heart with His love, rekindling each soul with Fire from above.[3]

A Two-Fold Plan for Revival

We cannot orchestrate revival, but we can lay the groundwork in two ways.

Pray for Revival Personally

First, pray the prayer in Psalm 85:6: "Will You not revive us again, that Your people may rejoice in You?" The Old Testament scribe Ezra wrote, "And now for a little while grace has been shown from the LORD our God, to leave us a remnant to escape, and to give us a peg in His holy place, that our God may enlighten our eyes and give us a measure of revival . . ." (Ezra 9:8). We must ask God to do the same for America and the world—to "give us a measure of revival."

Practice Revival Personally

Rededicate yourself to living in a perpetual state of revival personally. Revival happens one person at a time; we must let it begin with us. It is what the apostle Paul talked about when he said "be filled with the Spirit"—speaking, singing, giving thanks to God, submitting to one another in the fear of God (Ephesians 5:18–21). We can pray, "Revive us," but we should begin by praying, "Revive me!" Let us pray as did a hymnist of yesteryear: "Let the Holy Spirit come and take control, and send a great revival in my soul."[4]

Nine times in Psalm 119 the psalmist prays for revival (verses 25, 37, 40, 88, 107, 149, 154, 156, 159). Those would be excellent verses for every Christian to meditate upon as he or she seeks personal revival. If we are to change the world, we must first ask God to change us. When the flame is ignited in our heart we can pass the flame to others.

Begin today: Pray for, and practice, revival!

APPLICATION

I. Read 2 Chronicles 7:11–16.

   a. What was the occasion of this passage (verse 11)?

   b. What circumstance did God tell Solomon might occur in the future (verse 13)?

   c. Outline the steps God told Solomon the people should take (verse 14a):

- "will _____ themselves"
- "and _____ and _____ My face"
- "and _____ from their _____ ways"

   d. Outline the response God promised (verse 14b):

- "I will _____ from heaven"
- "will _____ their sin"
- "and _____ their land"

   e. Is God's promise of healing conditional or unconditional?

   f. Even though this promise was made to Israel, can the Church benefit from the principles found in this verse (1 John 1:9)?

g. What is the focus of God's judgment in verse 13? How is that a reversal of the blessings of the covenant (Deuteronomy 28:4–5, 8, 11–12)?

h. How does the promise of Deuteronomy 28:1–2 parallel with Galatians 6:7?

2. What direct action did King Josiah take to precipitate revival in Judah (2 Chronicles 34:3–7)?

a. Because Josiah was king, he could take these unilateral actions. How is America different in terms of government?

b. In a way, Josiah legislated revival in Judah. Why would that be harder in America?

c. Based on the history of revival in America, have revivals been from the top down or the bottom up?

d. Therefore, what is the power and responsibility of the individual Christian in bringing revival?

e. Do a rough calculation of the time gaps between major revivals in American history. Are we "due" for a revival now? Overdue?

3. How do the words of Ezra 9:8 apply to America today?

   a. In what sense has "grace" been shown to America?

   b. What might be God's purpose in that grace?

   c. What has to happen to the Church's "eyes"? What do we need to see?

   d. What could you pray for that might speed revival in America?

DID YOU KNOW?

Revival by definition means to restore something that previously existed—such as a strong Christian consensus in America. A monument to that original consensus was erected in 1889 in a park on Allerton Street in Plymouth, Massachusetts—the largest solid granite sculpture in the United States. It features a female figure personifying Faith, pointing toward heaven with her right hand while clutching a Bible with her left. On the four sides of the base are smaller statues representing Morality, Law, Education, and Liberty. Because of its obvious and strong Christian theme, the Park Service does not highlight the statue—another sign of the need for revival in America.

Notes
1. J. Edwin Orr, *Campus Aflame* (Glendale, CA: G/L Publications, 1971), 19.
2. Ibid., 110.
3. Vance Havner, *The Secret of Christian Joy* (Old Tappan, NJ: Fleming H. Revell Co., 1938), 24.
4. From the chorus of the hymn, "Send a Great Revival," by B. B. McKinney.

PART II

Is This the End for the World?

The Isolation of Israel

GENESIS 12:1–3

In this lesson we discover why the nation of Israel is a sign to the world.

OUTLINE

---

n the world of geo-eco-politics, it is not often that promises are kept over time. But a promise God made to Abraham more than 4,000 years ago is still in force. It is shaping our world today and will shape it even further as we approach the end of the age. God's promises are forever.

  I. **An Unconditional Covenant**

 II. **A Personal Covenant**

III. **A National Covenant**

 IV. **A Territorial Covenant**

  V. **A Reciprocal Covenant**

 VI. **A Universal Covenant**

VII. **An Eternal Covenant**

OVERVIEW

Most Israeli Jews, and many Jews living outside Israel, know someone who has been a victim of Palestinian terrorism in the Jewish homeland. Living with the prospect of death or injury due to Palestinian terrorism is a daily reality for Jews in Israel.

"Palestinians" is a generic term used to refer to Arabs who occupied the land of Palestine prior to 1948 and who were displaced when Israel was made a nation. Palestinians resent that displacement; they want their land back and they want Israel to be erased from the map. They want Jews either to be killed or to leave their land and live elsewhere in the world. Acts of terrorism are their ongoing effort to attack Israel's right to exist.

Israel is a tiny, 9,000-square mile island in a five-million-square mile sea of Arab nations that surround her. Her sixty-eight-year status as a legally reformed nation has resulted in a constant state of vigilance against attacks. Since the year 2000, an estimated 1,500 Israelis have been killed by Palestinian (Islamic) terrorists, and 8,000 Palestinians have died as a result of Israel's response to terror attacks. In spite of those unbalanced odds, the attacks against Israel continue.

In recent years, Palestinians have gained the sympathy of the world because Israel has built settlements on two percent of West Bank (Arab) land to create a buffer zone against Palestinian attacks and to create civil order in an otherwise chaotic region. But Israel has never been the aggressor in Arab-Israeli conflicts. Israel has been willing to find a two-state solution, making concessions to the Palestinians, but her offers are always rejected because they include Israel's right to exist as a nation.

Israel is fighting for her very existence. The subtitle of an article by *World* magazine editor Marvin Olasky succinctly summarizes Israel's dilemma: "Slammed if you do, dead if you don't." When Israel takes the tough but necessary measures to defend herself, she is slammed by world censure. If she fails to take those measures, she is attacked by hostile neighbors. In that article, Olasky filed this explanation of the impossible situation in which Israel finds herself today:

The Holocaust's 6 million murders led to the creation of the Israeli state in 1948 and the willingness of Jews to fight for it against enormous odds . . . . The hardened men and women who founded the state of Israel and fought to defend it in the 1950s, 1960s, and 1970s, became known for saying, "Never again." Never again would they make it easy for mass killers. Never again would they go down without a fight.

For several decades, non-Jewish Americans and Europeans understood that resolve. But then a generation grew up that did not know Adolf [Hitler]. Those without visceral awareness of the background saw Israelis not as victims trying to survive but as over-lords acting unjustly to poor Palestinians. Manipulators took the opportunity to re-package the old anti-Semitism as sympathy for an oppressed third-world population.[1]

Oppression and opposition to Jews is nothing new in world history. The descendants of Abraham were enslaved in Egypt for 400 years, then the ten northern tribes were captured by the Assyrians in 722 BC and the two south-ern tribes by the Babylonians in 586 BC. (Granted, these captivities were due to the Jews' sins.) Then Rome crushed the Jews in AD 70, dispersing them into the world where they lived for 1,878 years until the United Nations declared them a nation again in 1948. During the dispersion—the diaspora—more than six million Jews were exterminated by Hitler in the 1940s.

Only one factor can explain why the Jews still exist as a people and a nation: the promises of God. As God said through the prophet Ezekiel, He has preserved the Jews for His own name's sake: "'the nations shall know that I *am* the LORD,' says the Lord God, 'when I am hallowed *in you* before their eyes'" (Ezekiel 36:23, italics added). And through Isaiah God reminded the Jews that many of her hardships were discipline for her sins (Isaiah 40:2).

But discipline looks to a more righteous future. Why does God have a future for the Jews? Because of promises made to them in times past. The Jews represent a conundrum illustrated by the saying, "How odd of God, to choose the Jews."

It does seem odd from a human perspective. But there are two reasons God has preserved Israel as a nation: (1) because of a promise made to

Abraham, and (2) because of God's faithfulness to His Word. As we will see, nothing can cause God to break His promises to His people.

(The promise made to Abraham began in Genesis 12:1–3 and was re-affirmed several times to Abraham as well as his son, Isaac, and grandson, Jacob. Their descendants would be the inheritors of the promise God made to Abraham.) Genesis 12:1–3 is a cornerstone, a foundational block of Scripture on which a right understanding of the Bible rests. To disregard the promises God made to the father of the Jewish people is to be confused about biblical eschatology.

There are seven features of God's promise (God's covenant) in Genesis 12:1–3 that serve as mileposts in the journey from Genesis to Revelation.

An Unconditional Covenant

When God says "I will" (five times in Genesis 12:1–3), that signifies an uncon-ditional covenant. God is not asking Abraham to reciprocate; He is stating what He Himself will do for Abraham and his descendants. God confirmed the unconditional nature of this covenant in a unique ceremony in Genesis 15.

That ceremony was a common one in the ancient Near East. Sacrificial animals were cut in two and the parties to a covenant would walk between the pieces. They were saying, "May what happened to these animals happen to me if I break this covenant." But when God and Abraham conducted this ceremony, *God alone* walked between the pieces, taking full responsibility for the keeping of the covenant. This wasn't an agreement between equals; this was God promising to do something for Abraham and his descendants.

Paul Wilkinson notes that God alone signed and sealed the covenant, "since only He passed through the animal pieces. The inference drawn from Ancient Near Eastern custom is that in so doing, God invoked a curse upon Himself, should He ever break His promise."[2]

A Personal Covenant

God's promise to Abraham was personal: "I will bless you and make your name great" (Genesis 12:2). The personal pronouns *you* and *your* are used eleven times in verses 1–3. The promises have universal implications, but they began as personal promises to Abraham.

God directed Abraham to leave his home in Mesopotamia and settle in the rich and abundant land of Canaan (Exodus 3:8, 17; 13:5; 33:3). He prospered greatly and became wealthy with herds and servants (Genesis 14:14). The land of Canaan was promised to Abraham and his seed, a place where all his descendants could prosper as Abraham had done.

Abraham was revered in his own day as a powerful leader (Genesis 14:1–17) and is a pivotal figure in three world religions today: Judaism, Islam, and Christianity. The personal promise of the land to Abraham's descendants through Isaac and Jacob was never rescinded and remains in force today.

A National Covenant

Part of the promise to Abraham was that God would make a great nation from his descendants (Genesis 12:2a). In spite of the millions of Jews who have been killed through the centuries, the Jews are indeed a great nation. Professor Amnon Rubenstein gives us an impressive summary of Israel's national achievements:

> Minute in size, not much bigger than a sliver of Mediterranean coastline, [Israel] has withstood continuing Arab onslaughts, wars, boycott and terrorism; it has turned itself from a poor, rural country, to an industrial and post industrial powerhouse . . . it has reduced social, educational and health gaps between . . . Arabs and Jews. Some of its achievements are unprecedented: Israeli Arabs have a higher life-expectancy than most European whites; its democracy functions, inside Israel proper, in times of great national emergency . . . it has maintained freedom of the press in time of war; it stands out as a singular democratic, first-world island in a sea of Arab and Muslim poverty and backwardness.[3]

A Territorial Covenant

Land—a homeland—was part of God's promise to Abraham (Genesis 12:1): "To your descendants I have given this land, from the river of Egypt to the great river, the River Euphrates" (Genesis 15:18). From the Mediterranean coast on the west to the Euphrates River on the east; from Kadesh in the south (Ezekiel 48:28) to Hamath in the north (Ezekiel 48:1), Abraham was promised a huge grant of land—all of modern Israel, Lebanon, the West Bank of Jordan, and large parts of Syria, Iraq, and Saudi Arabia.

Because Israel has never occupied all that land, many scholars believe the promise of land should be spiritualized to refer to heaven instead of a literal homeland. But couldn't that promise have been made and fulfilled back in Abraham's previous homeland of Mesopotamia? Why travel all the way to Canaan to make a promise about heaven? No, this was a promise about literal land that will one day be fulfilled.

The promise was also reiterated to Abraham's son Isaac (Genesis 26:2–5) and Isaac's son Jacob (Genesis 28:13; 35:12)—and Jacob's descendants (Exodus 33:1–3). The land in this promise is the most important block of real estate in the world. As such, it will be the most hotly contested land in the world until Christ returns. Israel has been removed from the land three times (the Egyptian sojourn, the Assyrian and Babylonian captivities, the diaspora), but today she is back in the land. God has kept His promise to Abraham and his descendants.

The Old Testament is replete with God's promises, made through His prophets, about the land belonging to Israel forever: Jeremiah 32:37, 41; Ezekiel 11:17; 20:42; 34:13; 37:21, 25; 39:28; Amos 9:14–15. Taking these promises at face value is important. The last line of Amos 9:15, for example, says: "'And no longer shall they be pulled up from the land I have given them,' says the LORD your God." This could not apply to previous occupations of the land since they were removed. But the day is coming when they will never again be "pulled up from the land."

When the United Nations created a homeland for the Jews in 1948, they carved off a portion of what had historically been Israel's land—part of Judea and Samaria, now called the West Bank—and gave it to Palestinians. But when these same Palestinians and others attacked Israel in 1967 in the famous Six-Day War, Israel won that West Bank territory back. They didn't take it by aggression. They won it while defending themselves from attack—land that had been given to Abraham by God centuries earlier!

God cares for this land, His gift to Abraham (Deuteronomy 11:12). Israel regaining the central part of her homeland in 1948 is a sign for all who know biblical prophecy. It is an indication that we are moving into the period prior to the Second Coming of Israel's King.

A Reciprocal Covenant

God's promise to protect and bless Abraham had a corollary—a promise to bless those who bless Abraham and his descendants: "I will bless those who bless you, and I will curse him who curses you" (Genesis 12:3). It's very simple: Nations that bless Israel will be blessed; nations that curse Israel will be cursed.

The prophet Zechariah warned the nations that came against Israel: "for he who touches [Israel] touches the apple of His eye" (Zechariah 2:8). And he warns nations of the future the same way (Zechariah 9:8). The pages of history (and the Old Testament) are littered with the decline of nations that came against Israel. In ancient times, powerful peoples like Egypt, Midian, Moab, Babylon, and Greece were ruined as a result of raising their hand against Israel.

In the modern era, Communist Russia was dissolved and Nazi Germany was crushed. Perhaps the most dramatic example of God's protection was the aforementioned Six-Day War in 1967. The United Arab Republic, and the Jordanian, Syrian, and Palestinian armies attacked Israel from three directions. Although hopelessly outnumbered, Israel defeated all these nations and captured vast amounts of land including the Sinai Peninsula, the Golan Heights, the Gaza Strip, and the West Bank.

The most foolish thing any modern nation could do is to stand against Israel in its foreign policy.

A Universal Covenant

The universality of the covenant with Abraham reveals its most important purpose: "And in you [Abraham] all the families of the earth shall be blessed" (Genesis 12:3). The purpose of God's promise to Abraham was not to exclude the rest of humanity from God's blessing, but to ultimately include them! Abraham's descendants would be the rich repository of the knowledge of God that all humanity needs.

For example, almost all the writers of the Bible were Jewish. And most importantly, Jesus was a Jew—a descendant of Abraham, Isaac, and Jacob. Through "the blessing of Abraham" came a blessing for the Gentiles (the rest of humanity) in the person of Christ (Galatians 3:14). Finally, the land of Israel and city of Jerusalem exist because of the promises to Abraham being fulfilled through his descendants. It is to that land and city which the

King of kings and Lord of lords will one day return to judge the world and establish His kingdom on earth. The entire human race has been blessed by the promises of God to Abraham.

An Eternal Covenant

God's promise to Abraham came in three stages: initiated in Genesis 12:1–3, formalized in Genesis 15:1–21, and amplified in Genesis 17:1–18. In Genesis 17, Abraham is nearly 100 years old and God comes to him to affirm that the covenant is an "everlasting covenant" and the land of Canaan will be his descendants' "everlasting possession" (Genesis 17:7–8). That promise was affirmed graphically through the prophet Jeremiah: as long as the heavens and the foundations of the earth remain, so will God's faithfulness to Israel (Jeremiah 31:35–37; see also Psalm 105:8–9).

Particularly striking was the vision given to Ezekiel—dry bones (of Israel) coming back to life (Ezekiel 37:1–12). The dry bones represent the scattered nation of Israel being brought back to life and reunited to inherit the blessings of Abraham's covenant. That is what we are seeing today! But rebuilding the "bones" of the nation is not enough. Israel has not been

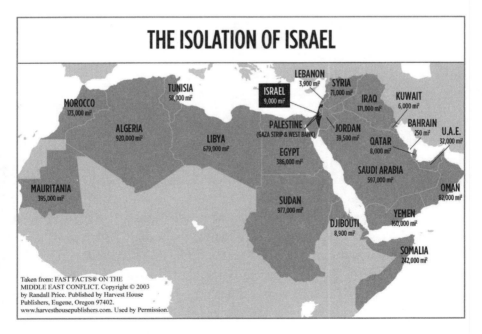

THE ISOLATION OF ISRAEL

Taken from: FAST FACTS® ON THE
MIDDLE EAST CONFLICT. Copyright © 2003
by Randall Price. Published by Harvest House
Publishers, Eugene, Oregon 97402.
www.harvesthousepublishers.com. Used by Permission.

made totally spiritually alive yet. But Ezekiel saw the breath (Spirit) of God coming into the resurrected physical bodies (Ezekiel 37:8–10) and that will happen (Zechariah 12:10; Romans 11:27–28).

Two prophecies are yet to be fulfilled: Israel needs to inhabit all the land promised to her and she needs to turn to her Messiah, Jesus Christ. But those will be fulfilled in God's time. Israel is indeed a sign to the world that God keeps His promises and the end of the age is approaching.

APPLICATION

---

1. Identify each of the components of God's covenant promise to Abraham in Genesis 12:2–3.

   a. I will make you a _____ _____.
      I will _____ you.
      [I will] make your _____ _____.
      You shall be a _____.
      I will _____ those who _____ you.
      I will _____ him who _____ you.
      In you all the _____ of the _____
         shall be blessed.

   b. If you were the leader of a nation on earth, what would your foreign policy toward Israel be in light of the promise of verse 3?

2. Read Ezekiel 36:22–23.

   a. What would be God's purpose in redeeming and restoring Israel (verse 22)?

   b. What had Israel (in Ezekiel's day) done to God's "holy name" (verses 22–23)?

c. What does the phrase "in you" in verse 23 say about Israel's restoration?

d. How does "in you" make the restoration of Israel a sign to the world about God (verse 23)?

e. How has the world responded to Israel's restoration to her homeland? Is the world seeing the sign?

f. When the nations gather against Israel at the end of the age, how will they finally understand the sign that is Israel (Ezekiel 39:1–8)?

3. Do you find the word "if" addressed to Abraham in Genesis 12:1–3?

a. What does that say about conditions Abraham must fulfill?

b. How many times does God say "I will"?

c. Who is taking responsibility for the fulfillment of these promises?

d. How is Deuteronomy 28:1 different from Genesis 12:1–3? What does "if you . . . God will" suggest about this covenant? Is it conditional or unconditional?

e. How does the conditional nature of this covenant justify the Assyrian and Babylonian captivities? What could Israel have done to avoid those unpleasant experiences?

f. Is Jesus' promise in John 15:7 conditional or unconditional? If conditional, what are the conditions? What is the promise?

4. In Deuteronomy 7:6–8, how might God's words to Israel in verses 7–8 also be applied to God's election of you to salvation in Christ (Ephesians 1:4–6)?

DID YOU KNOW?

The term "diaspora" comes from the Greek word *diaspora*, a dispersion or scattering. While it can refer to the scattering of any ethnic or racial group from their homeland, "the diaspora" most frequently refers to the scattering of Jews from Judea. Greek *diaspora* is used three times in the New Testament to refer to Jews living outside Judea as a result of the Assyrian and Babylonian captivities or persecution (John 7:35; James 1:1; 1 Peter 1:1). Many Jews who had believed in Jesus were driven from Jerusalem (Acts 8:1) and all Jews were scattered from the city when Roman armies destroyed it in AD 70. Though most Jews still live outside Israel, a return from the diaspora began in the first half of the twentieth century and continues today.

Notes

1. Marvin Olasky, "Israel at age 67: Slammed if you do, dead if you don't," *World*, April 21, 2015, http://www.worldmag.com/2015/04/ israel_at_age_67_slammed _if_ you_do_dead_if_you_ don_t. Accessed April 7, 2016.

2. Paul R. Wilkinson, *Understanding Christian Zionism: Israel's Place in the Purposes of God* (Bend OR: The Berean Call, 2013), 21.

3. Amnon Rubinstein, "Peace Won't Be Instant, but Can't Be Dropped," *JWeekly*, May 9, 2003, http://www.jweekly.com/article/full/19844/peace-won-t-be-instant-but-dream-can-t-be-dropped/.

The Insurgency of ISIS

In this lesson we uncover the history and goals of the radical Islamic group known as ISIS.

OUTLINE

No political agenda has changed the world as recently, quickly, and shockingly as radical Islamic terrorism. While ISIS is relatively new, its roots are deep in the geo-political history of the Middle East. Christians today must understand the goals of radical Islam and how to respond.

I. The Development of ISIS

II. The Description of ISIS
    A. Their Teachings
    B. Their Tradition
    C. Their Training
    D. Their Tactics

III. The Desires of ISIS
    A. Revival of the Caliphate
    B. Return of the Messiah

IV. **The Defeat of ISIS**
   A. Remember
   B. Reach Out
   C. Realize
   D. Radicalize
   E. Rely

OVERVIEW

When the members of the Virgin Mary Church in the village of Al-Our, Egypt, 150 miles south of Cairo, assembled, the group was smaller than usual. Just a few days earlier, in February 2015, the Islamic State of Iraq and Syria (ISIS) had decapitated thirteen of their members on a beach in Libya.

The thirteen were part of twenty Christians murdered by ISIS that day. These Coptic Christians had gone to Libya in search of work. But they were kidnapped by ISIS in December 2014, and held until they were executed in February. The men were given the opportunity to recant their Christian faith before they were killed. They all refused, going to their death with the name of Jesus on their lips.

These twenty Christian believers represent just a few who have fallen under the swords of ISIS. Many more, both men and women, have been shot, tortured, raped, forced into ISIS marriages, sold into sexual slavery, and driven from their villages to become refugees. ISIS has firmly established itself in Iraq and Syria, but its tentacles now reach into other nations of Asia, the Middle East, and Africa where its franchises commit the same atrocities.

Who and what is ISIS? How should we as Christians respond to this threat?

The Development of ISIS

Charting the evolution of the group known as ISIS helps us understand who they are.

- **AQI (Al-Qaeda in Iraq).** Osama bin Laden funded a branch of Al-Qaeda in Iraq in response to the 2003 invasion by America and other partners. Iraq was the birthplace of what became ISIS.

- **ISIS (Islamic State in Iraq and Syria).** The leaders of AQI moved from Baghdad into Syria to take advantage of the civil war there. Since 2014, ISIS has gained control over large swaths of northern Iraq and Syria. ISIS is the name by which the world learned of their radical movement.

- **ISIL (Islamic State in Iraq and the Levant).** As ISIS expanded its operation throughout 2014 and 2015, its name changed to ISIL—the Islamic State in Iraq and the Levant. "Levant" is an ancient designation for "Middle East" and reflects the expanding operations of ISIS.

- **DAESH (or Da'ish).** DAESH is an Arabic acronym meaning the same as ISIL. ISIL hates the name because, when pronounced, it sounds like a derogatory term in Arabic. Many critics and opponents of ISIS refer to them as DAESH in a mocking sense.

- **IS (Islamic State).** Islamic State is the current name and the name preferred by its own leaders for two reasons: First, it includes "Islam" and "state," which summarizes its goal of uniting the Muslim religion into a single, powerful political entity. Second, the new name drops the last two letters, I and S, thus eliminating geographical references that would suggest the organization is anything less than a worldwide movement.

ISIS as an organization is recent, but its history is ancient and complex. It involves the Soviet invasion of Afghanistan in the 1970s, the founding of Islam, and the ancient discord between Isaac and Ishmael, sons of Abraham.

In Genesis 12:1–3, God promised to make Abraham the father of a great nation, but he was 75 years old and did not have a male heir. So Abram's wife, Sarai, growing impatient, gave her maidservant to Abram as a surrogate to bear a child for the couple. Hagar, the servant, bore a son who was named Ishmael.

Even though Ishmael was not the legitimate child of promise, God told Abraham that Ishmael would be the father of multitudes (Genesis 17:20). Fourteen years later—fulfilling God's promise, when Abraham was 100 years old and Sarah was 90—they had a son named Isaac.

There was tension between Hagar and Sarah over their two sons and Sarah ultimately banished Hagar and Ishmael from their home. Ishmael fathered twelve sons who became the progenitors of the modern Arab peoples. Almost all Arabs, including Muhammad, the founder of Islam, revere Ishmael as the father of their race. Jews draw their lineage from Abraham, Isaac, and Jacob; Arabs draw theirs from Ishmael.

The historic Arab–Jewish conflict, simmering since 1948, can be traced back to the animosity between Ishmael and Isaac. But the ISIS-against-everybody conflict is not primarily racial but religious. Radical Islam's hatred of the Jews is both racial and religious. ISIS hates any person, Muslims and Arabs included, who does not subscribe to their radical Islamic beliefs. ISIS attacks Jews on both fronts: racial (Jews are not Arabs) and religious (Jews are not radical Muslims).

It is important to understand that most Muslims are not Arabs. There are large populations of non-Arabic Muslims in Turkey, Iran, and Indonesia. And not all Arabs are Muslims—there are Arab Christians as well as Arabs of other religions. Not even all members of ISIS are Arabs (though the majority are), but they are definitely all Islamic.

In summary, ISIS targets anyone whose religion differs from theirs or who occupies land that Islam previously conquered in the name of Allah.

While the roots of ISIS are ancient, the fruit is recent. Charles Dyer and Mark Tobey have provided the following five-part outline of ISIS's modern development.[1]

- **Stage 1: The Mujahideen**. In the 1970s, the Communist-leaning ruler of Afghanistan appealed to Moscow for help in quelling an uprising. Russia sent forces to invade Afghanistan and subdue the Islamic tribal factions. These conservative Afghans waged guerilla warfare (jihad) against the Russians and were called the mujahideen ("holy warriors"). Other mujahideen streamed into

Afghanistan from the Middle East to fight against the infidel Russian invaders—including Osama bin Laden. By 1988, the Russians withdrew, leaving Afghanistan in chaos.

- **Stage 2: The Taliban.** A war hero gathered a small group around him called Taliban ("the students"). The movement grew rapidly and by the late 1990s he gained control of the government. His goal was to make Afghanistan into a perfect Islamic state operating under sharia law. Osama bin Laden pledged his support to the Taliban.

- **Stage 3: Al-Qaeda.** In 1990, a U.S. led coalition entered Kuwait and drove out Saddam Hussein's Iraqi army (the First Gulf War). Osama bin Laden and the Taliban viewed this invasion much like the invasion of Afghanistan by Russia—an invasion of infidels into Muslim lands. Bin Laden founded Al-Qaeda ("the base") to begin attacking Western targets, which led to the September 11, 2001, terror attacks on the United States. Al-Qaeda under bin Laden became the world's highest profile terror organization.

- **Stage 4: Al-Qaeda in Iraq.** The U.S. invaded Afghanistan in search of bin Laden and Al-Qaeda who went into hiding. Al-Qaeda set up franchises in various Middle East locations, especially in Iraq after the capture of Saddam Hussein in 2003 by American and coalition forces. Al-Qaeda in Iraq became the most ruthless of all the Al-Qaeda branches. The leader of Al-Qaeda in Iraq was killed in 2006 and bin Laden was killed in 2011; President Obama declared victory over Al-Qaeda and an end to the war in Iraq. But that claim was premature.

- **Stage 5: ISIS.** Two sects vie for supremacy in Islam: Shiites and Sunnis. When America pulled out of Iraq, Shiites returned to power which re-animated the opposing Sunni Al-Qaeda forces. When civil war broke out in Syria, Al-Qaeda (which had become ISIS—the Islamic State in Iraq and Syria) moved from Baghdad to Syria to fight against Syrian president Assad's Shiite government.

And they brought ruthless terrorist tactics with them: beheading, rape, selling women into sexual slavery, persecuting homosexuals, and mutilating violators of sharia law. Syrians fled to escape. The leader of ISIS broke away from Al-Qaeda and announced himself head of ISIS and of a new Islamic caliphate. As of this writing, ISIS's forces have come under attack by American and other militaries intent on stopping their expansion.

The Description of ISIS

The following profile will set ISIS apart from the beliefs of the majority of the world's Muslims.

Their Teachings

ISIS's goal is to return Islam to the pure teachings of the Quran and Hadith—a voluminous collection of Muhammad's teachings and activities while he was the caliph (ruler) of Islam. ISIS takes literally teachings concerning jihad against infidels, hatred of Jews and Christians, subjugation of women, lifestyle regulations, and conquering of territory for Allah.

Their Tradition

In September 2014, President Obama said that ISIS is not Islamic.[2] But ISIS would disagree. ISIS is perhaps the purest form of Muhammad's Islam on the planet, desiring to eliminate everyone who doesn't submit to Allah as God according to their understanding. And the notion that Islam is a religion of peace is not found in its earliest history. Muhammad himself conducted scores of military wars in his expansion of the religion. Within two centuries after its founding, Islam ruled territory from the Atlantic shores to India. By its warring tactics, ISIS has simply renewed Muhammad's original strategies of expansion.

Their Training

ISIS is a guerilla army, not a conventional army. They recruit adults and children into their army through mosques and Muslim community centers in Syria. These institutions are indoctrination and recruitment centers where ISIS teaches its radical version of Islam. In Raqqa, Syria, the headquarters of ISIS, they run the city government with fully functioning courts and religious leaders who walk the streets to ensure compliance with sharia law. ISIS pays the parents of pre-teen boys who join the military a monthly stipend. These "Caliphate Cubs" are sent to sharia camps for indoctrination, then to military training camps. Boys who excel are sent into battle or on suicide missions; others are sent back into their communities to act as spies and informants.

Their Tactics

ISIS's tactics are the same as Muhammad's: conquer, plunder, suppress non-Muslims (by conversion, taxation, death, or emigration), and rule. Their goal is a worldwide caliphate, or Islamic government. It has a sophisticated social media presence on the Internet and an impressive public relations strategy.

Besides ISIS, other like-minded radical Islamic groups are pursuing similar goals. For example, the century-old Muslim Brotherhood, based in Egypt, has branches in eighty countries. They have written strategies to infiltrate and undermine the governments and cultures of Western nations like Britain and the United States—what they call gradualism: a gradual, non-violent takeover of non-Muslim countries. Western leaders who think the threat of radical Islam is confined to the Middle East will be in for a rude awakening.

The brutal tactics of ISIS are well-documented. Unlike Jesus, who said His followers would be known by their love (John 13:35), ISIS is known for brutality akin to the Assyrian kingdom of old whose armies struck fear into the hearts of other nations. And they do it all in the name of their religion, Islam.

What motivates ISIS? What religious beliefs have stoked their mission?

The Desires of ISIS

ISIS is looking for the return of their Mahdi ("messiah") and his rule over a worldwide Islamic kingdom. Everything ISIS is doing now is preparatory for those events. ISIS believes that the escalation of war will hasten a final apocalypse which will hasten the return of the Mahdi. Indeed, ISIS wants war because it plays into their end-times eschatology.

Revival of the Caliphate

In preparation for the apocalypse and worldwide caliphate, ISIS wants to retake, for starters, all the land that belonged to the last Islamic caliphate, the Ottoman Empire. That empire was dissolved following World War I and the territory divided into (roughly) the Middle Eastern nations we see today.

The nearest expression of an Islamic theocracy today is Iran. Its government is elected but it is run behind the scenes by Muslim clerics called the Guardian Council. The head of this council, the Supreme Leader, can override the elected officials at will as the Iranian constitution specifies. ISIS's capital in Raqqa, Syria, paints a picture of how life in an ISIS-like caliphate would look: sharia law with quick judgment for any violations.

Return of the Messiah

Both Sunni and Shiite Muslims look for the return of the Muslim messiah and generally agree on these end-time events: a final apocalypse between Islam and infidels at Dabiq, Syria, where Islam will be victorious; a false messiah; the return of Jesus (or Isa, held by Islam as a prophet) who defeats the false messiah; the return of the true messiah, or Mahdi; the establishment of the worldwide caliphate. Radical Muslims view violence as a good thing—it hastens the end-time events.

The Defeat of ISIS

Islam is the second-largest, but fastest-growing, religion in the world. Christians must come to grips with the fact that part of modern Islam is radical, bent on the subjugation of all who disagree with it. How should we respond?

Remember

The principle of Hebrews 13:3 applies here: "Remember the prisoners as if chained with them—those who are mistreated—since you yourselves are in the body also." We must pray for the persecuted Church that is suffering under ISIS. We must stand with them in unity (Ephesians 4:4–6) and empathy (Romans 12:15).

Reach Out

As hard as it is, we are responsible to love our enemies (Matthew 5:44) and pray for their salvation. We must demonstrate the love of Christ in order to reveal the Christ of love. Loving our Muslim friends and neighbors will show them that we belong to Jesus (John 13:35). Muslims honor Jesus as a great prophet; we have the opportunity to manifest Him as a great Savior, Lord, and friend.

Realize

The battles of this earth are actually battles in spiritual places and must be fought with spiritual weapons (2 Corinthians 10:3-4; Ephesians 6:12; 1 John 3:8; 5:19). God put civil governments in place on earth to protect the good from the evil (Romans 13:1-4). And sometimes those governments call citizens to war in defense of an orderly civil society. We must always fight on our knees and sometimes with our hands. The Church has for centuries embraced the teachings of Augustine and Aquinas who defended the "just war" theory.

Radicalize

We must not let Muslim or other extremists own the word "radical." Loving one's enemies, laying down one's life for friends, is far more radical than terrorism. Jesus was the most radical human who ever lived and we must be radical as His followers. If ISIS is willing to die for their wrong beliefs, how much more willing should we be to die for the truth of the Gospel (Luke 14:27)? Jesus despises apathy and indifference (Revelation 3:16). We must take the Gospel fearlessly into our neighborhoods and the world to preach the love of Christ.

Rely

ISIS cannot destroy the Church (Matthew 16:18). It continues to grow. We must rely on the purpose, power, and promises of God.

We do not know what the future holds in the Middle East or in the West. But we do know who holds the future. While we wait for the day when swords will be beat into plowshares and spears into pruning hooks (Isaiah 2:4), let us faithfully represent Christ to all who do not yet know Him—even to those who are the enemies of His Church.

APPLICATION

---

1. In Genesis 12:1–3, what was the central promise God made to Abraham (verse 2a)?

   a. What would that nation be to all the world (verse 3b)?

   b. How is every nation related to the Jews, either for good or ill (verse 3a)?

   c. In light of the promise in verse 3a, what is the ultimate destiny of the nations in the Middle East who are against Israel?

2. What did the angel of the Lord tell Hagar about the son she would bear, Ishmael (Genesis 16:11–12)?

   a. How has that prophecy played out in the tensions between Arabs and Jews?

   b. What promise did God make to Abraham about Ishmael (Genesis 17:20)?

   c. To whom did the covenant promises of Genesis 12:1–3 pass (Genesis 17:21)?

    d. By the time of Ishmael's death, how was the prophecy of the angel of the Lord (Genesis 16:12) being played out (Genesis 25:13–18, especially verse 18)?

    e. _____ are descended from Isaac while _____ are descended from Ishmael.

3. From your reading of this lesson, explain the two reasons ISIS hates the Jews:

    a. The racial reason:

    The religious reason:

    b. Explain why not all Arabs are Muslims and why not all Muslims are Arabs.

4. ISIS now calls themselves IS—the Islamic State. Explain why both terms are accurate:

    a. Islamic: (are they Islamic?)

    b. State: (what kind of state do they want?)

5. How does Hebrews 13:3 apply to our perspective on Christians persecuted by ISIS?

a. How does Romans 12:15 apply?

b. How are Ephesians 4:4 and 1 Corinthians 12:12 the basis for our identity with suffering Christians?

6. What is the best way to show anyone—especially our Muslim friends and neighbors—that we are true followers of Jesus (John 13:35)?

7. Explain what each of the following verses say about the spiritual origin of earthly battles:

a. 2 Corinthians 10:3–4

b. Ephesians 6:12

c. 1 John 3:8

d. 1 John 5:19

8. As mentioned in this lesson, explain the radical Islamic notion of "gradualism."

DID YOU KNOW?

The story at the beginning of this lesson recounts the execution of twenty Christians by ISIS in Libya. There were actually 21. An African named Matthew Ayairga was kidnapped along with the other 20, but he was not a Christian at all. It is unclear why ISIS included him in the group of Christians they rounded up. But ISIS demanded the same thing from Matthew as they had from the others: Reject the Christian Christ or die. Matthew, having observed the faith of the other twenty men, decided that what they believed must be real. He confessed to his ISIS captors, "Their God is my God." And so, he too was executed. He entered Paradise that day much like the thief on the cross who believed moments before he died (Luke 23:39–43). But that was enough.

Notes

1. Charles H. Dyer and Mark Tobey, *The ISIS Crisis: What You Really Need to Know* (Chicago, IL: Moody Publishers, 2015), 32–44.
2. Ashley Killough, "Strong Reaction to Obama Statement: 'ISIL Is Not Islamic,'" CNN Politics, http://www.cnn.com/2014/09/10/politics/obama-isil-not-islamic/.

LESSON 8

The Resurrection of Russia

E Z E K I E L   3 8 – 3 9

In this lesson we discover what the future holds for Russia.

O U T L I N E

After World War II, the world had two superpowers: the United States and the Soviet Union. When the Soviet Union collapsed in 1991, Russia took a backseat in world affairs. But Russia is back, inserting herself in world affairs. Ezekiel saw her rise and coming demise centuries ago.

I. The Russian Aggression
   A. The Language Argument
   B. The Location Argument

II. The Russian Alliance
   A. The Commander of the Alliance
   B. The Countries in the Alliance

III. The Russian Attack
   A. Why Will Russia and Her Allies Attack Israel?
   B. Where Will the Russian Invasion Occur?
   C. When Will the Russian Invasion Occur?

IV. The Russian Annihilation
  A. Monumental Convulsion
  B. Military Confusion
  C. Major Contagion
  D. Multiple Calamities

V. The Russian Aftermath
  A. The Birds and the Beasts
  B. The Burnings
  C. The Burials

OVERVIEW

One of the biggest news stories of 2014 was the Russian invasion and annexation of Crimea, a peninsula on the southern coast of the republic of Ukraine. Crimea has a centuries-old connection to Russia and Russia wanted it back. So they took it. There was marginal opposition from Ukraine who was trying to manage internal turmoil of its own. The international community objected, but nobody opposed Russia. And Crimea is now back in Russian hands. This was a blatant display of Russian power by its president, Vladimir Putin.

Since the annexation of Crimea, Putin has also led Russia to sell air defense systems to Israel's chief enemy, Iran, and has come to the defense of Syrian President Bashir al-Assad, with airstrikes against rebels seeking to topple the dictator. Putin's intervention in Syria was ostensibly to suppress ISIS forces, but it soon became apparent Russia was there in support of long-time ally Assad.

None who know the history of Vladimir Putin, the hardline KGB operative who rose to become president of Russia, are surprised at his aggressive geo-political moves. The dissolution of the Soviet Union in 1991 was a rebuke and an embarrassment to Soviets like Putin. Most analysts believe Putin's recent aggression has one goal: to return the former Soviet Union, if not to its former Communist political structure, then at least to its role as a superpower on the world stage.

The Cold War (1947–1991) was won by the United States as signaled by the dissolution of the Union of Soviet Socialist Republics. Sensing a lack of American will on the international stage in recent years, Russia is testing all observers as it moves to center stage in world politics.

What does the future hold for Russia? Putin obviously wants to be recognized as the leader of a world power and he should not be taken lightly. In fact, we can say with biblical certainty that he will move Russia into a pivotal place of power in the last days. The prophet Ezekiel gives us a detailed picture of Russia's rise and ultimate demise.

The Russian Aggression

Ezekiel 38–39 describes the future invasion of Israel by Russia and a coalition of mostly Islamic nations. The prophecy begins with ten proper names (Ezekiel 38:1–6). The first, Gog (verse 2), is the name of a man, followed by the names of nine nations that will form an end-times alliance with Gog against Israel: Magog, Rosh, Meshech, Tubal, Persia, Ethiopia, Libya, Gomer, and Togarmah (verses 2–6). We find Russia at the head of the alliance. Ezekiel's two-chapter prophecy is the most detailed prophecy of war in the entire Bible.

"Russia" as a name doesn't appear in the Bible. But the name "Rosh" in Ezekiel's list refers to the nation ruled by the leader of the coalition. There are two strong reasons for believing "Rosh" refers to Russia.

The Language Argument

"Rosh" occurs in Ezekiel 38:2–3 and 39:1. It is a Hebrew word that means "head, top, or summit." It's easy to note the phonetic similarity between Rosh and Russia. The great Hebrew lexicographer, Wilhelm Gesenius, wrote that "Rosh" is "undoubtedly the Russians, who are mentioned by the Byzantine writers of the tenth century, under the name *the Ros*."[1]

The Location Argument

Ezekiel, along with ancient Jewish rabbis, saw Jerusalem as the center of the earth (literally, the "navel" of the earth—see "midst" in Ezekiel 5:5). This means that Jerusalem was the center of the compass. In Scripture, north means north of Jerusalem, south means south of Jerusalem, and so forth.

Both Daniel and Ezekiel saw the ruler who would lead an attack against Israel in the latter days as coming from "the North" (Daniel 11:5–35) or "far north" (Ezekiel 38:6, 15). If one draws an arrow due north starting from Jerusalem, the arrow stops in modern Russia. Russia alone occupies the giant land mass in the "far north" from Jerusalem.

The Russian Alliance

If Russia is the leader of the alliance that makes war against Israel, who are the other nations?

The Commander of the Alliance

Gog is "the prince of Rosh, Meshech, and Tubal" (Ezekiel 38:2). Several times in these chapters Gog (high or supreme) is spoken to as if to a person. "Gog" may be a title like President or Pharaoh rather than a name. Gog is from the land of Magog, but he also rules Rosh, Meshech, and Tubal (Ezekiel 38:3). Gog is commanded by God to "be a guard" for these other nations (verse 7). "Guard" suggests that Gog is the commander and protector of the members of the alliance.

The Countries in the Alliance

Along with Rosh, these nations or lands are also listed by Ezekiel.

Magog

Gog is from the land of Magog (verse 2). Magog was a grandson of Noah (Genesis 10:2) and many scholars believe his descendants settled around the Black and Caspian seas on Russia's southern border. In *The Jeremiah Study Bible,* I identify this region as home to the former "-stan" nations (Kazakhstan, Kyrgyzstan, and so on), all former satellites of the Soviet Union. What unites the sixty million residents of this region today is their religion: Islam.

Meshech and Tubal

Meshech and Tubal were also grandsons of Noah (Genesis 10:2). The descendants of these two men established cities or territories bearing their names. C. I. Scofield identifies Meshech as "Moscow" and Tubal as

"Tobolsk."[2] But many other scholars and experts identify them as territories in modern Turkey.

Persia

Persia is mentioned in Ezekiel 38:5 and about 35 more times in Scripture. Persia became Iran in 1935, then the Islamic Republic of Iran in 1979. Today, Russia is Iran's strongest ally and Israel's strongest enemy.

The 2015 agreement negotiated by President Obama with Iran, allowing them to pursue a path to nuclear weapons, has confounded allies and enemies alike. Not to mention unfreezing more than $100 billion in assets—a pure gift to the world's leading financier of terrorism! Iran despises America and Israel with equal fervor. The nuclear deal, when it expires, will instantly catapult Iran onto the nuclear stage since her research infrastructure was left intact by the deal. And the money Iran receives in the deal will only aid her ability to become a bad actor in the region. Russia and Iran will become intimate bedfellows when it comes to moving against Israel in the latter days.

Ethiopia

Ethiopia (Ezekiel 38:5) is one of two North African nations that will join the alliance, approaching from Israel's south. Ethiopia was founded by Cush, another grandson of Noah (Genesis 10:6), and originally represented the land south of Egypt. Today that region is the modern country of Sudan, another declared enemy of Israel.

Libya

Libya is the only nation on Ezekiel's list that retains its ancient name today. Founded by Put, another of Noah's grandsons (Genesis 10:6), Libya is the land west of Egypt. Today, Libya is another of Russia's Islamic-nation friends.

Libya's longtime dictator, Muammar Gaddafi, was overthrown in the Arab Spring uprisings in 2011. Since then, the country has been in political turmoil. But there is evidence that Libya is seeking to purchase military armaments from Russia.[3]

Gomer

Gomer, a grandson of Noah (Genesis 10:2–3), has a name that strikes a chord with the modern name "Germany" according to some scholars.

Nobody needs to remind the world of Germany's history with the Jewish people in World War II. If Germany becomes part of an alliance with Russia against Israel, it would not be the first time anti-Semitism has played a part in her history.

Togarmah

Togarmah was a great-grandson of Noah (Genesis 10:3). Ezekiel helpfully locates this people in "the far north" (Ezekiel 38:6). Could Togarmah be the foundation of the modern nation of Turkey, as some believe?

Regardless of their exact modern identities, these nine peoples were identified as parts of an alliance led by Gog, the leader, to come against Israel. Russia and Turkey will lead from the north, joined by Iran from the east and Sudan and Libya from the south—and possibly Germany from the west. Ezekiel says there will be "many peoples" with Gog (Ezekiel 38:9) so there may be other nations in the alliance as well—possibly the "-stan" nations from the former Soviet bloc.

The Russian Attack

Ezekiel goes on to describe the actual invasion of Israel (Ezekiel 38:7–17). But remember: Ezekiel is prophesying *against* Gog. When God says, "I am against you" (verse 3), the "you" is Gog, not Israel. God is the speaker in this prophecy, through Ezekiel against Gog.

We now need to answer the why, where, and when questions about this invasion.

Why Will Russia and Her Allies Attack Israel?

From Russia's perspective, there are three reasons. First, the alliance will come to seize Israel's land (Ezekiel 38:11–12). Second, they will come to *steal* Israel's wealth (Ezekiel 38:12–13). Third, they will come to slaughter Israel's people (Ezekiel 38:11–12, 16). This *slaughter* will be the culmination of the Arab hatred for Israel that has been simmering since the days of Ishmael and Isaac (Genesis 21:8–19).

Where Will the Russian Invasion Occur?

It will be in the land of those who have been regathered from the nations and are dwelling safely: the land of Israel (Ezekiel 38:8). Ezekiel confirms

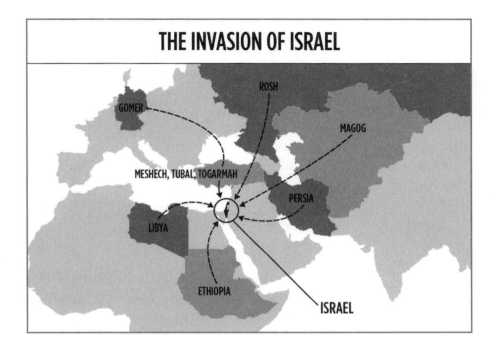

THE INVASION OF ISRAEL

this numerous times in chapter 38. This will be a lopsided invasion! Russia is 785 times larger than Israel in terms of land. Add in the size of the other alliance members and the odds are overwhelmingly against Israel.

When Will the Russian Invasion Occur?

Two of three events that will precede the invasion have already happened, but the third will occur in due time. The events are:

1. Israel Must Be Present in Her Land

Ezekiel makes this point clearly in 36:24; 38:8, 12; 39:25, 27–28. Prior to 1948, the Jews as a nation had not been in the land since AD 70 when they were driven out by the Romans who destroyed everything, making the land uninhabitable. After World War II, persecuted European Jews began pouring into Israel and the United Nations declared Israel a nation in May 1948. Hundreds of thousands of Jews from all over the world began streaming into their homeland. Just under half of the Jews in the world today live in Israel.

An important note about the progress of Ezekiel's prophecy: Ezekiel 36–37 describes the regathering of Israel; Ezekiel 38–39 describes the invasion of Israel; Ezekiel 40–48 describes Israel in the Millennium. So the invasion of Israel takes place between the regathering and the Millennium. That is, between the *national* and the *spiritual* rebirth of the nation.

2. Israel Must Be Prosperous in Her Land

Ezekiel 36:11 describes the growth and prosperity of Israel when she is back in her land, and that has certainly been fulfilled. Indeed, Israel's wealth is one of the reasons for the invasion by the Russian alliance. By all standard measures—technology, innovation, start-up companies, education, wealthy citizens—Israel surpasses all countries of her size in the world and many that are much larger.

3. Israel Must Be Peaceful in Her Land

This is the condition that remains to be realized: peace in the land. Ezekiel 38:8, 11, and 14 suggest that Israel thinks she is secure, that there is no need for strong defenses. Something unusual must happen to make this embattled nation think she is secure—and the prophet Daniel tells us what it will be: the Antichrist will establish a peace treaty that protects Israel (Daniel 9:27). Because of peace between Arabs and Israelis, Israel will feel secure. But she will also be a ripe target for an unexpected invasion. The Antichrist's peace treaty will begin the seven-year Tribulation period. So that is when the invasion of the Russian alliance will happen.

The Russian Annihilation

The alliance will come upon Israel "like a cloud, to cover the land" (Ezekiel 38:15–16). There is no human way Israel could survive. And yet she will because God will intervene (Ezekiel 38:18–19).

In addition to the three reasons for the invasion I mentioned previously, there is a fourth: to set the stage for judgment against Russia and other nations that have a history of rebelling against God (Ezekiel 39:7–8). "Then the nations shall know that I am the LORD, the Holy One in Israel" (verse 7). God will allow the greed and hatred of the alliance to be a reason for the judgment they deserve. It will be a destruction such as the world has never seen.

Monumental Convulsion

There will be unrivaled earthquakes and destruction. The entire earth will feel the reverberations of God's destruction of the armies (Ezekiel 38:19–20).

Military Confusion

In the midst of the destruction, the invading armies will turn on each other in confusion (Ezekiel 38:21). This will parallel what happened to the enemies of Judah in the days of King Jehoshaphat (2 Chronicles 20:22–25).

Major Contagion

Because of the myriad of dead bodies, disease will break out resulting in further chaos and judgment (Ezekiel 38:22).

Multiple Calamities

There will be natural disasters: "flooding rain, great hailstones, fire, and brimstone" (Ezekiel 38:22), similar to what happened at Sodom and Gomorrah.

All these judgments will extend to the homelands of the alliance nations (Ezekiel 39:6). It is not just the armies that will be judged but the populations of their nations as well.

The Russian Aftermath

The disposal of the bodies and equipment of the invaders will be monumental (Ezekiel 39).

The Birds and the Beasts

The scavengers of the animal kingdom will be called by God to help dispose of rotting corpses (Ezekiel 39:17–20). God calls it a "sacrificial meal" (verse 17).

The Burnings

Equipment—tons and tons of it—will have to be burned, scrapped, recycled, and otherwise disposed of (Ezekiel 39:9–10). Ezekiel describes weapons of his day because that's all he knew. But instead of swords, shields, bows, and arrows being destroyed, it will be modern military hardware.

The Burials

It will take Israel "seven months" to bury what remains of the dead in a place called "the Valley of Hamon Gog" (Ezekiel 39:11–12).

Two things will happen in this terrible conflict: a rebellious coalition of nations will be judged, and God will prove His faithfulness to His people Israel. As always, those who purpose to rise against God are themselves taken down. Those who choose to sow violence reap a harvest of greater violence and destruction (Galatians 6:7).

Five times in Ezekiel 38 and 39, God repeats His desire to make His name known among the nations (38:16, 23; 39:6–7, 23). This is not egotistical on God's part. Rather, it is for our benefit. God doesn't need to know how great His name is, but we do. His faithfulness—His greatness—is just another way for us to realize who He is.

We live in a world beset by trouble and tribulation among nations. And there is certainly trouble yet to come. But God is in control. He uses even the sins of the nations to accomplish His purposes, making His name known and drawing mankind to Himself.

APPLICATION

---

1. How do we know that a spiritual rebirth is coming for the nation of Israel (Ezekiel 36:24–28; 37:14, 26–27)? What will be its characteristics?

2. To whom is the prophecy of Ezekiel 38–39 directed (Ezekiel 38:3; 39:1)?

a. How many nations or peoples will join with Gog to come against Israel?
   List their names (Ezekiel 38:2–3, 5–6).

b. Who is going to lead these nations against Israel (Ezekiel 38:3–4)?

c. What does "hooks into your jaws" (verse 4) suggest about God's power
   and control over these nations?

d. How does God "whistling" to call Assyria to punish Israel compare with
   His sending the Russian alliance (Isaiah 5:26; 7:18).

e. What does this say about God's control of the nations (Job 12:23; Daniel
   2:21; Acts 17:26–27)?

f. What does "be a guard for them" mean for Gog? What is his role in the
   alliance (Ezekiel 38:7)?

g. Geographically, what is the connection between "far north" (Ezekiel
   38:6, 15) and Russia from Jerusalem's point of view?

h. Ezekiel wrote his prophecy while in captivity in Babylon. Check a map—
   what modern country is directly "far north" of Babylon?

3. Why is Ezekiel 38:8 a good description of the nation of Israel in both
   Ezekiel's day and our day? (See also 36:3.)

a. How did Ezekiel portray the nation in the vision he saw in Ezekiel 37:1–14?

b. What time indicator is given in Ezekiel 38:8? How do we know this invasion hasn't already happened? ("After _____ days . . . in the _____ years.")

4. Based on information from this lesson, give the "big idea" of these sections of Ezekiel:

   a. Ezekiel 36–37: the _____ of Israel
   b. Ezekiel 38–39: the _____ of Israel
   c. Ezekiel 40–48: the _____ of Israel

5. Based on size and numbers, why would the coming Russian invasion of Israel be a certain victory for the alliance, humanly speaking?

   a. Who saves Israel? Why (Ezekiel 39:7)?

   b. What comfort do you take from this prophecy concerning future world events? Who is in charge?

DID YOU KNOW?

According to Orthodox Church tradition, the disciple Andrew first brought the Gospel to the region of Belarus, Russia, and Ukraine. The baptism of Vladimir the Great and his family in Kiev in AD 988 marks the official beginning of Christianity in Russia and the beginning of the Russian Orthodox Church which is in full communion with the Eastern

Orthodox Church. Prior to the Bolshevik Revolution in Russia in 1917, Christianity was the dominant religion of Russia. After 1917, the Union of Soviet Socialist Republics became officially atheistic based on the teachings of Marx and Lenin. Since the fall of the Soviet Union in 1991, the Russian Orthodox Church has gradually gained restored freedom while maintaining its distance from the state.

Notes

1. S. P. Tregelles, *Gesenius' Hebrew-Chaldee Lexicon* (Grand Rapids, MI: Eerdmans, 1957), 752.
2. C. I. Scofield, *The Scofield Study Bible* (New York: Oxford University Press, 1909), 883.
3. Mustafa Fetouri, "Libya Looks to Russia for Arms," *Al-Monitor*, April 20, 2015, http://www. al-monitor.com/pulse/originals/2015/04/libya-us-uk-france-russia-uneast-west-armament-deal-morocco.html.

LESSON 9

The Rapture of the Redeemed

1 THESSALONIANS 4:13-18

In this lesson we define and discover the details of the coming event known as the Rapture.

OUTLINE

As He prepared to leave this world, Jesus told His disciples He would return and take them to the place He had prepared for them. Later, the apostle Paul provided the details of this event. Since it could happen at any time, the Rapture is a strong motivation for a consecrated, expectant life.

   I. The Rapture Is a "Signless" Event

  II. The Rapture Is a Surprise Event

 III. The Rapture Is a Sudden Event

  IV. The Rapture Is a Selective Event

   V. The Rapture Is a Spectacular Event
   A. The Sound of the Lord's Command
   B. The Sound of Michael's Voice
   C. The Sound of the Trumpet

VI. The Rapture Is a Sequential Event
  A. The Return
  B. The Resurrection
  C. The Redemption
  D. The Rapture and the Reunion

VII. The Rapture Is a Strengthening Event
  A. Expectation
  B. Consecration
  C. Examination

OVERVIEW

Two publishing events have helped insert the Rapture of the Church into cultural conversations around the world. First was *The Late Great Planet Earth*, written by Hal Lindsey, and released in 1970. Estimates are that this book has sold more than 35 million copies.

The second event was the 12-volume series of books known as "The Left Behind Series," *Left Behind* being the title of the first volume that was released in 1995. The books were co-authored by Tim LaHaye and Jerry Jenkins. So far, the 12-volume series has sold more than 62 million copies. The ninth volume, *Desecration*, was released shortly after the terror attacks of September 11, 2001, and sold enough copies before the end of the year to be the world's bestselling book of that year.

These authors have done the Church a great service by reminding her of the incredible importance of the prophetic Scriptures. The Rapture is perhaps the most important piece of prophecy for today's Christians to understand since it could very well impact them personally.

In this lesson, we will discover what the Rapture is, defend it biblically, and explain its personal and practical importance for the Christian.

In summary, the Rapture is an event where all who have put their trust in Christ, living and deceased, will suddenly be caught up from earth, be joined with Christ in the air, and taken to heaven. Paul describes the Rapture in 1 Thessalonians 4:13–18.

"Rapture" is not a biblical word. It is derived from the Latin translation of 1 Thessalonians 4:17, which translates Greek *harpazo* (to catch up or carry away) as *rapiemur* from the Latin *rapio*. The Greek *harpazo* occurs thirteen times in the New Testament with four variations of meaning, each of which contributes to understanding what Paul is describing in verse 17: "Then we who are alive *and* remain shall be caught up together with [the dead] in the clouds to meet the Lord in the air."

First, *harpazo* can mean "to carry off by force." Christ will use His power to remove living and deceased believers from the last enemy, death.

Second, *harpazo* can mean "to claim for oneself eagerly." Christ purchased us with His blood and so will return to claim those who are His.

Third, *harpazo* can mean "to snatch away speedily." The Rapture will occur "in the twinkling of an eye" (1 Corinthians 15:52).

Fourth, *harpazo* can mean "to rescue from the danger of destruction." This meaning supports the idea that the Rapture will save the Church from the danger of the seven-year Tribulation.

This coming event is part one of Christ's two-part return to earth. First, to remove the Church from the world. Second, seven years later, to establish His kingdom on earth. For every prophecy in Scripture about Christ's first advent there are eight about His second.[1] The 216 chapters of the New Testament contain 318 references to the Second Coming of Christ.[2]

Will the Rapture occur at Christ's Second Coming? The short answer is, "Yes, but . . ." The Rapture sets in motion the end-time events leading to Christ's Second Coming. The two stages—Rapture and Return—will be separated by a seven-year Tribulation on earth. The purpose of the Rapture is to spare Christ's own from the horrors of the Tribulation according to Revelation 3:10.

The physical return of Christ will happen at the end of the Tribulation as described in vivid detail in Revelation 19. The apostle John's vision of Christ's return echoes what Zechariah saw in the Old Testament: a giant battle, Christ returning to the Mount of Olives, bringing His saints with Him (Zechariah 14:1, 3–5). Jude states what will happen when Christ returns: judgment of the ungodly (Jude 14–15).

The prophets saw what appears to be the Tribulation—"the time of Jacob's trouble" (Jeremiah 30:7)—not the Rapture. But that is not surprising;

they didn't differentiate clearly between the First and Second Advents of Christ. The prophets "inquired and searched carefully" (1 Peter 1:10–11), but saw more of the big picture than the details. And they didn't see the Church at all, which is who the Rapture affects. The prophets saw the future like seeing successive mountain peaks through a telephoto lens. They saw the peaks (events), but not the distance that separates them.

Three New Testament passages tell us about the Rapture: John 14:1–3; 1 Corinthians 15:50–57; 1 Thessalonians 4:13–18. Paul's words in 1 Thessalonians are the most complete and form the basis for this lesson.

First, we must note that Paul gained his understanding of the Rapture via special revelation from God—he called it a "mystery" in 1 Corinthians 15:51, meaning a truth not previously revealed. The revelation was "by the word of the Lord" (1 Thessalonians 4:15).

Second, Paul passed on the content of this revelation to meet a practical concern of the Christians in Thessalonica. They were concerned about the fate of Christians who died before Christ's Second Coming (1 Thessalonians 4:13–18) and about the timing of the Rapture—whether it had already happened (2 Thessalonians 2:1–2).

Now—seven characteristics of the Rapture.

The Rapture Is a "Signless" Event

Unlike the Second Coming, no signs will precede the Rapture. It could occur at any moment. This is called the doctrine of *imminency*—that is, the Rapture is imminent; it could happen at any moment. Specifically, nothing in God's prophetic program must take place as a prerequisite to the Rapture. Things *may* happen but nothing *must* happen. That means we don't know when it could happen. It could be today or years from today.

Bible expositor A. T. Pierson wrote, "Imminence is the combination of two conditions, viz., certainty and uncertainty. By an imminent event we mean one which is certain to occur at some time, uncertain at what time."[3]

Without any warning, Jesus Christ will return to rapture His saints and take them to heaven. Christians must live "prepared lives," ready to meet their Savior at any moment.

The Rapture Is a Surprise Event

While many through the years have predicted the date of the Rapture and Jesus' Second Coming, Jesus' words in Matthew 24:36–39 should be taken literally: No one, including Jesus and the angels, knows the time of His return. Only God the Father knows. Not knowing when Jesus will come for His Church causes us to be ready at all times.

The Rapture Is a Sudden Event

Paul wrote that the Rapture will take place "in a moment, in the twinkling of an eye" (1 Corinthians 15:52). The Greek word behind "moment" is *atomos*, from which we get the English word "atom." *Atomos* referred to something indivisible. In terms of time, it's like saying it will happen in the briefest moment of time possible: in an instant; in a flash.

The Rapture Is a Selective Event

All three of the major passages that teach about the Rapture make it clear that it involves believers only (including innocent children too young to believe). In John 14:1–3, Jesus is speaking to His disciples who are obviously believers. His words, "I will come again and receive you to Myself" are what we call the Rapture—the reuniting of Jesus Christ with His faithful followers.

In 1 Corinthians 15 Paul talks about "those who are Christ's at His coming" (verse 23). He concludes the passage by talking about their abounding in the work of the Lord (verse 58), an obvious reference to Christian believers.

Three times in 1 Thessalonians 4:13–18 he refers to believers as "brethren" (verse 13), as those who "believe that Jesus died and rose again" (verse 14), and as the "dead in Christ" (verse 16). The question is this: Were Jesus and Paul talking about you? Will you be a participant in the Rapture?

The Rapture Is a Spectacular Event

The actual Second Coming of Christ is described as a glorious event in Revelation 19:11–14—and rightly so. For that reason, the Rapture has traditionally played second fiddle to the Second Coming. But the Rapture itself will be a spectacular event.

One verse is all we need: "For the Lord Himself will descend from heaven with a shout, with the voice of an archangel, and with the trumpet of God" (1 Thessalonians 4:16). I used to think these are not three distinct sounds but one sound described three different ways. I have since rethought that position.

The Sound of the Lord's Command
Jesus will shout for believers to rise from the grave and come from the earth just as He called forth Lazarus from the grave (John 11:43).

The Sound of Michael's Voice
The archangel's voice is that of Michael, the only archangel identified in Scripture (Daniel 12:1; Jude 9). Michael is God's warring angel which suggests his role in the Rapture. There is an invisible war going on around us (Ephesians 6:12). The image here is of God's mighty, warring angel coming to ensure the safety and freedom of Christ's souls as they meet Him in the air. Michael's shout may be a call to God's hosts of angels to come to serve as escorts for the Church as they move from earth to heaven.

The Sound of the Trumpet
This is the same trumpet Paul refers to as "the last trumpet" in 1 Corinthians 15:52. In Roman military terminology, the last trumpet of the morning dispersed soldiers to their duty for the day. In that sense, the last trumpet of Christ sends believers to their ultimate service for Christ: joining Him in heaven.

Based purely on how the Rapture will sound—voice, shout, trumpet—it will be a spectacular event.

The Rapture Is a Sequential Event

In 1 Thessalonians 4, Paul identifies three sequential events that will happen at the Rapture.

The Return
The initiating event is Christ's return from heaven (verse 16a). This fulfills the prophecy given by the angels the day Christ ascended into heaven—that

the disciples would see Him return in like manner (Acts 1:11). Jesus ascended; Jesus will return. The same person who left earth will return.

The Resurrection
"The dead in Christ will rise first" (verse 16). "Sleep" is a biblical metaphor for death (John 11:11; Acts 7:60; 13:36). Those who have been "asleep" in Christ will be "awakened" and raised from the dead. How bodies dead for centuries, not to mention bodies that have been cremated or destroyed in explosions, will be recomposed and raised, we do not know. But they will be.

The Redemption
Following the resurrection of the dead, believers who are alive will rise to meet Christ in the air. They will experience the same physical transformation as the deceased, then resurrected, believers. Paul says in 1 Corinthians 15:51–52, "We shall not all sleep, but we shall all be changed—in a moment, in the twinkling of an eye, at the last trumpet." We will become like Christ's resurrected, glorified body, fit for heaven.

The Rapture and the Reunion
Three reunions will take place (verse 17).

First, dead bodies will reunite with their spirits which Christ will have brought with Him from heaven (verse 14). Deceased bodies will be reunited with their spirits.

Second, resurrected believers will meet living believers. It will be a reunion of saints from every era of history, uniting finally as the one, universal Church.

Third, together these groups will experience the joy of reunion with their Lord. They met Him first at their conversion, now they meet Him face to face.

Translating living saints to heaven has happened before the Rapture. In fact, four raptures have already occurred. In the Old Testament, Enoch was taken to heaven without dying (Genesis 5:24), as was Elijah (2 Kings 2:1, 11). We have already mentioned Christ being taken up to heaven (Acts 1:11), and the apostle Paul also was taken up to "the third heaven" and returned to earth (2 Corinthians 12:2–4).

There are two raptures that are yet to occur. During the Tribulation, God's two witnesses will be taken to heaven without first dying (Revelation 11:12). The primary Rapture yet to occur, of course, is the Rapture of the Church just before the beginning of the Tribulation.

The Rapture Is a Strengthening Event

The Rapture can change our life; it is a source of personal comfort and hope. The reason Paul wrote to the Thessalonians about it was to ease their concerns about their departed loved ones. Death is not final. The resurrection of believers who have died will reverse the effects of death. All who have lost loved ones to the sting of death can be comforted in the knowledge that they will see them again. But it is also a source of strength. Jesus promised His disciples, on the night He was arrested, that He would return for them (John 14:1–3).

It is no wonder that Paul told the Thessalonians to comfort themselves with the truth concerning the Rapture (1 Thessalonians 4:18).

The Rapture can impact our life now, in three ways, while we wait for it to happen.

Expectation

The letter from Paul to Titus puts in words how the expectation of the Rapture should impact our life:

> For the grace of God that brings salvation has appeared to all men, teaching us that, denying ungodliness and worldly lusts, we should live soberly and righteously in the present age, looking for the blessed hope and glorious appearing of our great God and Savior Jesus Christ, who gave Himself for us, that He might redeem us from every lawless deed and purify for Himself His own special people, zealous for good works (Titus 2:11–14).

Consecration

I am told that Robert Murray M'Cheyne, a brilliant young Scottish preacher who died at age 29 in 1843, wore a wristwatch with the words "The Night Cometh" engraved on its face. Every time he checked his watch he was

THE RAPTURE	THE RETURN (SECOND COMING)
Christ comes in the air (1 Thessalonians 4:16–17)	Christ comes to the earth (Zechariah 14:4)
Christ comes for His saints (1 Thessalonians 4:16–17)	Christ comes with His saints (1 Thessalonians 3:13; Jude 1:14)
Believers depart the earth (1 Thessalonians 4:16–17)	Unbelievers are taken away (Matthew 24:37–41)
Christ claims His bride	Christ comes with His bride
Christ gathers His own (1 Thessalonians 4:16–17)	Angels gather the elect (Matthew 24:31)
Christ comes to reward (1 Thessalonians 4:16–17)	Christ comes to judge (Matthew 25:31–46)
Not in the Old Testament (1 Corinthians 15:51)	Predicted often in the Old Testament
There are no signs. It is imminent.	Portended by many signs (Matthew 24:4–29)
It is a time of blessing and comfort (1 Thessalonians 4:17–18)	It is a time of destruction and judgment (2 Thessalonians 2:8–12)
Involves believers only (John 14:1–3; 1 Corinthians 15:51–55; 1 Thessalonians 4:13–18)	Involves Israel and the Gentile nations (Matthew 24:1–25:46)
Will occur in a moment, in the time it takes to blink. Only His own will see Him (1 Corinthians 15:51–52)	Will be visible to the entire world (Matthew 24:27; Revelation 1:7)
Tribulation begins	Millennium begins
Christ comes as the bright morning star (Revelation 22:16)	Christ comes as the Sun of Righteousness (Malachi 4:2)

Some content taken from *THE END*, by Mark Hitchcock. Copyright © 2012. Used by permission of Tyndale House Publishers, Inc. All rights reserved. www.tyndaledirect.com.

reminded that time is marching on. We won't always have time to win souls to Christ and to consecrate our own lives for His service. The apostle John exhorted his readers to "not be ashamed before Him at His coming" (1 John 2:28). The any-moment, imminent return of Jesus for His Church is life's greatest stimulus for living a consecrated life.

Examination

Jesus warned that He is "coming quickly" (Revelation 22:12). That means we should live every day as if He was coming that day. But will we be ready?

Will we be found with heart and hands dedicated to serving Him at the moment we see Him face to face? Even more important, have we committed ourselves by faith to Christ so we are assured of being part of His Church that is called into His presence at the Rapture? When the voice, the trumpet, and the shout are heard there will be no opportunity to make a decision. Be sure today that you have said yes to Christ so you will be prepared to rejoice at His appearing.

APPLICATION

I. Read John 14:1–4.

    a. Why were the disciples "troubled" (see John 13:33, 36)?

    b. How much did they seem to understand about where Jesus was going?

    c. What promise did Jesus make them (see John 13:36b)?

    d. Check different translations for "mansions" in verse 2. What word(s) could also be used? What is Jesus implying about "many rooms"?

    e. What is Jesus' ultimate goal for His disciples? To prepare a place separate for them or a place with Him (verse 3)?

    f. How is the Rapture a fulfillment of His ultimate goal of reuniting Himself with His followers? (See the last words of 1 Thessalonians 4:17.)

g. You have been serving a Savior you've never seen. What does it mean to you to know you will one day be united with Him?

2. Read 1 Thessalonians 4:13–18.

a. What two concerns did Paul have for the Thessalonians as evidenced by the words "ignorant" and "sorrow"? How does ignorance lead to sorrow (verse 13)?

b. How is verse 14 consistent with what Paul wrote in Romans 6:5, 8?

c. When did Paul receive the doctrine ("by the word of the Lord," verse 15) he is teaching the Thessalonians? (See 2 Corinthians 12:1–4 and the gap in Paul's life indicated by Galatians 1:17–2:1.)

d. What three sounds will be heard at the time of the Rapture (verse 16a)?

e. What will happen first in response to these sounds (verse 16b)?

f. What will happen next? (See "then" in verse 17.)

g. How does the word "always" (verse 17) address the concerns the disciples had in John 13:36–14:1?

h. How do Paul's words take the "sting" out of death? (See 1 Corinthians 15:54–55.)

3. Read 1 Corinthians 15:50–58.

   a. What was the definition of "mystery" given in this lesson (verse 51)?

   b. How does that definition apply here? Did the Corinthians already know this information?

   c. How quickly will the transformation at the Rapture take place (verse 52)?

   d. What is Paul's final exhortation in light of not needing to worry about death (verse 58)?

DID YOU KNOW?

Predicting the date of the Rapture and/or Second Coming has been a popular pastime for years among Bible students. The most recent was when radio evangelist Harold Camping predicted the Rapture would occur on May 21, 2011. He had earlier predicted that the event would take place on September 6, 1994. When the 2011 date came and went with no Rapture, he moved the date forward to October 21. On that date, Camping said, God would destroy the universe. If you are reading these words you have a good idea that Camping was wrong in his prediction. If anyone says they know the date of Jesus' return, they know something not even Jesus knew (Matthew 24:36–39).

Notes

1. "The Second Coming of Christ," *preceptaustin.org.*, February 21, 2015, www.preceptaustin.org/the_second_coming_of_Christ.htm.

2. Chuck Swindoll, "Does the Bible Teach that Jesus Will Return?" *Jesus.org*, n.d., www.jesus.org/early-church-history/promise-of-the-second-coming/does-the-bible-teach-that-jesus-will-return.html.

3. Arthur T. Pierson, *Our Lord's Second Coming as a Motive to World-Wide Evangelism* (Published by John Wanamaker, n.d.). Quoted by Renald Showers in *Maranatha—Our Lord, Come!* (Bellmawr, NJ: The Friends of Israel Gospel Ministry, Inc., 1995), 127.

Translated Before the Tribulation

SELECTED SCRIPTURES

*In this lesson the believer gains assurance that
they will not face the coming Tribulation.*

OUTLINE

The events of the coming age are not impossible to decipher. There are differing opinions about the timing of the Tribulation, but specific aspects of the Tribulation are not debatable. The Tribulation is a time of both purification and punishment, and it is fitting with a God who displays both love and justice.

I. The Picture of the Tribulation
    A. The Surprise of the Tribulation
    B. The Severity of the Tribulation

II. The Purpose of the Tribulation
    A. The Tribulation Will Purify Israel
    B. The Tribulation Will Punish Sinners

III. The Perspectives on the Tribulation

IV. **The Protection from the Tribulation**
   A. Our Protection Is Affirmed by Christ's Promise
   B. Our Protection Is in Accord with Biblical Precedent
   C. Our Protection Is Apparent in the Book of Revelation
   D. Our Protection Is Assured by God's Love
   E. Our Protection Is Accomplished by Christ's Sacrifice

OVERVIEW

Predictions of impending catastrophes have terrified people through-out history. Most of them have been false. So how can we tell the false predictions from the real?

One sound measure of prophetic accuracy is the predictor's track re-cord. By this measure, the Bible has no competitor. Every event prophesied in the Bible has occurred except those remaining to be fulfilled in the end times. The flood of Noah, the famine in Egypt, the captivity of the Jews, and the destruction of Jerusalem come immediately to mind. The Bible's record of 100 percent accuracy in prophesying events of the past gives us absolute confidence in the fulfillment of those it prophesies to occur in the future.

One of the most persistent prophecies of a catastrophe yet to come concerns what Bible scholars call the *Tribulation*—a period filled with un-precedented horrors, upheavals, persecutions, natural disasters, massive slaughter, and political turmoil in the years immediately prior to Christ's Second Coming. All who accept the authority of the Bible believe the Tribulation will occur. And the spiraling chaos of today's world leads many to fear that it may be upon us, and they might soon be trapped in that horrific period with no way of escape.

The Picture of the Tribulation

I have found that many people wonder just what the Tribulation is, or even what the word means. Most of us are aware of it only because of its use in the Bible. *Tribulation* translates from the Greek *thlipsis*, a term designating the giant weight used to crush grain into flour. So the idea behind tribulation is utterly crushing, pulverizing, or grinding a substance into powder.

Its most common use today is as a technical term to designate a specific, traumatic event prophesied in the Bible to occur at an unspecified time in the future. That event—the Tribulation—is one of the prominent features of the prophetic end times.

The Surprise of the Tribulation

In his letter to the church in Thessalonica, the apostle Paul describes the event that will signal the beginning of the Tribulation period (see 1 Thessalonians 4:13–18). We call this initiating event the Rapture of the Church—the moment when Christ appears, raises the godly dead, and draws living Christians from the earth to be with Him.

The next natural question for Paul's readers would have been, "When will this happen?" Paul anticipates the question and begins chapter 5 with these words: "But concerning the times and the seasons, brethren, you have no need that I should write to you. For you yourselves know perfectly that the day of the Lord so comes as a thief in the night" (1 Thessalonians 5:1–2).

We are not given the ETA of the Rapture. It will come upon us unexpectedly, and the Tribulation will follow immediately in its wake.

The Severity of the Tribulation

Nowhere in all Scripture will you find one word or description that says anything good about the Tribulation period. Moses called it "The day of their calamity" (Deuteronomy 32:35). Zephaniah said it was "The day of the Lord's anger" (Zephaniah 2:2). Paul referred to it as "The wrath to come" (1 Thessalonians 1:10). John called it "The hour of trial" (Revelation 3:10), and "The hour of His judgment" (Revelation 14:7). Daniel described it as "A time of trouble, such as never was since there was a nation" (Daniel 12:1).

Jesus tells us that the Tribulation will be a time of terror and horror without precedent. "For then there will be great tribulation, such as has not been since the beginning of the world until this time, no, nor ever shall be. And unless those days were shortened, no flesh would be saved; but for the elect's sake those days will be shortened" (Matthew 24:21–22).

The central chapters of Revelation give us a vivid description of the horrors of the Tribulation period. Great wars will ravage the world as nations rise up lusting for conquest. All peace will end, and rampant slaughter will bloody the earth. A quarter of the world's population will die from war, starvation, and beastly predators. Everyone from national leaders to servants and slaves will flee the cities to hide in caves and under rocks (Revelation 6:2–17; 8:8–13; 9:1–20; 16:1–21).

To make matters even worse, a maniacal despot known as the Antichrist will rise to power. He will be multiple times more demonic than Antiochus, Nero, Stalin, and Hitler combined. He will demand total allegiance to his satanically inspired program, and those who resist will be barred from buying or selling food or any other product. His lust for power will not cease until the entire civilized world chokes in his tyrannical grasp (Revelation 13:1–18).

It is not an overstatement to say that the Tribulation will be hell on earth.

The Purpose of the Tribulation

The Tribulation is brought on earth by man's increasing rebellion and rampant sin. But God's hand will be heavily involved, just as it was when He brought the plagues on the rebellious nation of Egypt. The Tribulation is a planned program designed to accomplish two important goals.

The Tribulation Will Purify Israel

The Jewish nation exists as a product of God's promise to Abraham that his seed would be as numerous as the stars in heaven and would endure throughout all eternity (Genesis 12:1–3). The Jewish nation has tested God's patience throughout the many centuries of its existence, turning away from Him time and time again. But in spite of Israel's persistent rebellion, God will keep His promise, not only because He is God and does not break promises, but also because of His deep love for Israel.

The first purpose of the Tribulation is to purge out the Jewish rebels and bring about the final conversion of the nation. The Tribulation will be the fire that purifies Israel by burning out all the dross and impurities. As the prophet Ezekiel said, "I will make you pass under the rod . . . I will purge the rebels from among you, and those who transgress against Me" (Ezekiel 20:37–38).

The Tribulation Will Punish Sinners

The overall purpose of the Tribulation is to execute God's wrath upon those who oppose Him—first upon the Jews who have rebelled, as we have shown above, and then upon the rebellious Gentiles. "For the wrath of God is revealed from heaven against all ungodliness and unrighteousness of men, who suppress the truth in unrighteousness" (Romans 1:18).

We like to think and speak about the love of God, but not so much about His wrath. But wrath goes hand in hand with judgment, and it is as much an expression of His goodness as His love. In fact, love and wrath are two sides of the same coin.

If God's wrath does not accomplish the goal of purging—that is, if the rebellious person remains hardened and unrepentant—God still must protect the good. But He now has no alternative but to destroy those who insist on clinging to evil.

To sum it up, the overall purpose of the seven-year Tribulation period is to expose unregenerate people, both Jews and Gentiles, to the wrath of God. Just as the sun hardens clay and softens butter, God's wrath will harden some hearts and soften others. This shows us that the purpose of the Tribulation includes both conversion and punishment, depending essentially on how the objects of God's wrath respond to it.

The Perspectives on the Tribulation

How will the Tribulation affect the Church? Scholars of biblical prophecy answer this question in different ways. There are three basic viewpoints, each of which places the tribulation at a different point in time.

Posttribulationism, as the word itself indicates, teaches that the Rapture of the Church will occur after the seven-year Tribulation Period. This means Christians will be left on earth to endure all the terrors of the Tribulation along with the unbelievers. They will be taken up to be with Christ when the Tribulation ends at His Second Coming.

Midtribulationism teaches that the Church will be Raptured at the halfway point of the seven-year Tribulation period. In this view, Christians escape the last three-and-one-half years of it, which is when the very worst of the Tribulation disasters will occur.

Pretribulationism teaches that the Rapture takes place before the Tribulation. This means the Church will be removed from the earth before the Tribulation begins, sparing Christians from enduring any part of the seven-year barrage of God's wrath to be poured out upon the earth.

The Protection from the Tribulation

I firmly believe that *Pretribulationism* is the accurate perspective on the timing of end-time events. This means the Church will not suffer any of the terrible miseries of the Tribulation. The Bible gives us five reasons why believers can be assured of God's protection from this coming onslaught of His wrath.

Our Protection Is Affirmed by Christ's Promise

The clearest teaching on the believers' deliverance from the Tribulation comes to us from Christ's letter to the church in the Asia Minor city of Philadelphia: "Because you have kept My command to persevere, I also will keep you from the hour of trial which shall come upon the whole world, to test those who dwell on the earth" (Revelation 3:10).

1. The Promise Is Comprehensive

This promise goes much further than merely protecting believers from the devastation and misery going on around them. Jesus's promise goes further: Believers will not even be *in* the Tribulation, nor will they have to go *through* it. He tells us that the Church will be kept "from the hour of trial."

2. The Promise Is Clear

The fact that Christ promised to keep the Church from "the hour of trial" is highly significant. God knows that if He left His Church on earth, even though He protected us from actual harm, we would be deeply grieved by the suffering and devastation around us. Therefore, in His mercy and love, when the Tribulation comes He will remove us from the scene entirely.

Our Protection Is in Accord with Biblical Precedent

Throughout Scripture we see God protecting His people by removing them prior to His judgment against the evil that surrounded them. Noah and his family were safely enclosed within the ark before the judgment of the flood. Lot and his family were taken out of Sodom before judgment destroyed Sodom and Gomorrah. In addition, the Israelite spies were safely out of Jericho before judgment fell on that city.

It is easy to see the consistent pattern presented in these examples: God rescues the righteous before punishing the wicked. He allows the righteous and the wicked to live together in the world prior to judgment, as Jesus explained in the parable of the farmer allowing weeds to grow together with his wheat. But when harvest time comes, the wheat will be separated out before the weeds are cast into the fire (see Matthew 13:24–30).

Our Protection Is Apparent in the Book of Revelation

You have probably heard that the book of Revelation is the most difficult and confusing book in the entire Bible. But if you let it, Revelation will do the interpreting for you because it is, in fact, a self-interpreting book. The first chapter gives us an outline of its entire structure. Here we have the outline—the headings of the three major sections of the book: the things you have seen, the things which are, and the things that are to come.

1. **"The things which you have seen."** This short section covers Revelation 1:1–20. Here we have the record of the vision John saw while on the isle of Patmos. He tells of worshipping on the Lord's day when he heard the blast of a trumpet and turned to see the glorious figure of Christ, which he describes in magnificent detail. Christ speaks and explains the meaning of the symbols surrounding Him.

2. **"The things which are."** This section includes the next two chapters, Revelation 2 and 3, which contain seven letters to the seven churches of Asia Minor. John served as the primary leader of these churches before his exile to Patmos. These chapters deal with the "things which are." Each letter describes the spiritual health of a given church, accompanied by commendations, reprimands, warnings, and rebukes.

3. **"The things which will take place after this."** This section begins with Revelation 4 and continues through the end of the book. These chapters detail events that will take place in the future. Almost everything in Revelation 4–19 has to do with the Tribulation, describing in great detail the pouring out of God's wrath upon the earth.

Do you know what is conspicuously absent from these Tribulation chapters? The Church. The word *Church* appears nineteen times in Revelation 1–3, but it is not mentioned once in Revelation 4–19. Why? Because the Church is not there. It is no longer on the earth. Believers have been removed from the Tribulation and taken into heaven.

Our Protection Is Assured by God's Love

Paul assures his readers that once they become Christians, they have no more need to fear God's judgment: "There is therefore now no condemnation to those who are in Christ Jesus" (Romans 8:1). We have learned already that part of the purpose of the Tribulation is to execute God's wrath on those who reject Him. By simple logic, then, we can see why believers are to be spared the Tribulation. Their rebellion has been forgiven, and they have no need to be purged of it or punished for it.

When God put Jesus on the cross, He exacted from Him the full penalty due for our sin. We have nothing left to pay. But if we who have been cleansed by the blood of Christ are put through the Tribulation, which is a time of punitive judgment from God, it would mean that the price that Christ paid on the cross was not enough—that we still need the additional penalty of God's punitive wrath. The whole idea negates the efficacy of Christ's sacrifice for our sins.

Our Protection Is Accomplished by Christ's Sacrifice

What qualifies us to escape the traumas of the Tribulation? We can say that being a Christian, following Christ, submitting our lives to Him, or trusting Him as our Savior qualifies us. Christ is our Savior because He paid an enormous price to save us from the eternal doom we deserved because of our sin. We accept that gift by putting our trust in Him, and when we make that commitment, He accepts us as His own. That is what it means to be

His Church—to be those He will exempt from the wrath of the Tribulation and bring into heaven with Him.

The time is coming and now looms on the horizon when it will be too late. When the Tribulation arrives and God's people are taken into heaven, the door will close on those who have heard and rejected the Gospel. God's grace is available to rescue you from that wrath, so there is no need to despair. But there is a sense of urgency to His offer. Act now and you need have no concern about being caught in the Tribulation.

APPLICATION

I. Read Matthew 13:36–43.

    a. This is one of the few times where Jesus explained the symbolism of His parable. Write out the roles of all the players in this drama, what they are, and who they represent. (verses 37–39)

    b. When does the harvest occur? What could be another term for this time period (verse 39)?

    c. What does the burning of the tares represent? Is this symbolism literal? Explain (verse 40).

    d. What role do angels play in the end times (verses 39, 41)?

    e. Who will the angels gather? What will happen to those people (verses 41–42)?

f. What will allow the righteous to shine? How does that correlate with what you have learned about the Tribulation in this study?

2. Read Matthew 24:15–22.

   a. Verse 16 gives what advice to those at the start of the Tribulation? Why do you think that is?

   b. Verses 17 and 18 give advice to NOT do what in light of the Tribulation? Explain why.

   c. Who will be especially vulnerable and miserable during those days (verse 19)?

   d. What does verse 21 say about the severity of the Tribulation?

   e. If the Tribulation were longer than its proclaimed seven years, what does verse 22 say would happen?

3. Read 1 Thessalonians 4:13–18.

   a. Ignorance about the Second Coming could lead to what (verse 13)? Why should this especially not be a mark of Christians?

   b. Why (specifically) do we have hope for believers in Christ who have died (verse 14)?

c. What event does verse 16 describe? How does verse 16 explain the timing set forth in verse 15?

d. Who will meet the Lord? Where will they meet Jesus? For how long (verse 17)?

e. Why should this passage be a source of comfort for Christians, especially in light of the Tribulation?

DID YOU KNOW?

The writer of the book of Revelation was the beloved disciple, John. During a time of Christian persecution, they sent John to the island of Patmos as an exile. While there, he received a vision recorded for us in the book of Revelation. We know this because John noted his location in Revelation 1:9. Patmos is in fact a small island in the Aegean Sea. It is part of Greece, directly off the west coast of Turkey. It is a beautiful and idyllic place, one that you can still visit today.

Leader's Guide

Thank you for your willingness to lead a group through *People Are Asking . . . Is This the End?* The rewards of being a leader are different from those of participating, and as you lead you will find your own walk with Jesus deepened by this experience. During the ten lessons in this study, your group will explore ten major developments that signal a significant shift in the moral, spiritual, and geo-political landscape of the United States and the world—all of which beg the question, "Is this the end?" Your group will examine what the Bible has to say about these events and how you should respond as followers of Christ. There are several elements in this leader's guide that will help you as you structure your study and reflection time, so be sure to follow along and take advantage of each one.

Before You Begin

Before your first meeting, make sure the group members have a copy of the study guide so they can follow along and have their answers written out ahead of time. Alternately, you can hand out the guides at your first meeting and give the members time to look over the material and ask any preliminary questions. When possible, use the guide with the corresponding audio series. You can assign the study guide lesson as homework prior to the group meeting and then use the time to listen to Dr. Jeremiah's teaching and discuss the lesson.

During your first meeting, be sure to send a sheet around the room and have the members write down their name, phone number, and email address so you can keep in touch with them during the week. Keep in mind the ideal size for a group is between eight to ten people, which ensures everyone will have time to participate in discussions. If you have more people, break up the main group into smaller subgroups. Encourage those who show up at the first meeting to commit to attending the duration of the study, as this will help the group members get to know each other, create stability, and help you know how to prepare.

Each lesson begins with an outline of the material that will be covered followed by the reading. As you begin your group time, consider opening with an "icebreaker" question to get the group members thinking about the topic you will discuss. Ask people to share their initial thoughts on the subject, but ask them to keep the answers brief. Ideally, you want everyone in the group to get a chance to answer the question, so try to keep the responses to a minute or less. If you have talkative group members, make sure to state up front that everyone needs to limit his or her answer to one minute.

Give the group members a chance to answer, but tell them to feel free to pass if they wish. With the rest of the study, it's generally not a good idea to have everyone answer every question—a free-flowing discussion is more desirable. But with an opening icebreaker question, you can go around the circle. Encourage shy people to share, but don't force them.

Before your first meeting, let the group members know how the lessons are broken down. During your group discussion time the participants will be drawing on the answers they wrote to the applications questions, so encourage them to always complete these ahead of time. Also invite them to bring any questions and insights they uncovered while reading to your next meeting, especially if they had a breakthrough moment or didn't understand something.

Weekly Preparation

As the leader, there are a few things you should do to prepare for each meeting:

- *Decide whether you will play the audio series during the group time.* If you plan on playing the message from Dr. Jeremiah as part of the meeting, you will need to adjust the group time accordingly (see the next section for options).

- *Read through the lesson.* This will help you to become familiar with the content and know how to structure the discussion times.

If you do not plan on using the audio message during the meeting, you will need to prepare a brief summary of the material covered in the overview so everyone is prepared and ready to discuss the questions in the application section.

- *Decide which questions you want to discuss.* Depending on how you structure your group time, you may not be able to cover every question in the application section. So select the questions ahead of time that you absolutely want the group to discuss in depth.

- *Be familiar with the questions you want to discuss.* When the group meets you will be watching the clock, so make sure you are familiar with the Bible study questions you have selected. You can then spend time in the passage again when the group meets. In this way, you'll ensure you have the passage more deeply in your mind than your group members.

- *Pray for your group.* Pray for your group members throughout the week and ask God to lead them as they study His Word.

- *Bring extra supplies to your meeting.* The group members should bring their own pens for writing notes, but it's a good idea to have extras available for those who forget. You may also want to bring paper and additional Bibles.

Note that in many cases there will be no one "right" answer to the question. Answers will vary, especially when the group members are being asked to share their personal experiences.

Structuring the Discussion Time

You will need to determine with your group how long you want to meet each week so you can plan your time accordingly. Generally, most groups like to meet for either sixty minutes or ninety minutes, so you could use one of the following schedules:

Option 1 (Listen to Audio CD)	60 Minutes	90 Minutes
WELCOME: Members arrive and get settled	5 minutes	5 minutes
ICEBREAKER: Discuss an opening icebreaker-type question with the group	N/A	15 minutes
MESSAGE: Listen to the audio CD	40 minutes	40 minutes
DISCUSSION: Discuss application questions	10 minutes	20 minutes
PRAYER: Pray together as a group and dismiss	5 minutes	10 minutes

Option 2 (No Audio CD)	60 Minutes	90 Minutes
WELCOME: Members arrive and get settled	10 minutes	15 minutes
ICEBREAKER: Discuss an opening icebreaker-type question with the group	10 minutes	15 minutes
MESSAGE: Review the overview section	20 minutes	25 minutes
DISCUSSION: Discuss application questions	15 minutes	25 minutes
PRAYER: Pray together as a group and dismiss	5 minutes	10 minutes

As the group leader, it is up to you to keep track of the time and keep things moving along according to your schedule. You might want to set a timer for each segment so both you and the group members know when your time is up. (Note there are some good phone apps for timers that play a chime instead of a disruptive noise.) Don't feel pressured to cover every question you have selected if the group has a good discussion going. Again, it's not necessary to go around the circle and make everyone share.

Don't be concerned if the group members are quiet or slow to share. People are often quiet when they are pulling together their ideas, and this might be a new experience for them. Just ask a question and let it hang in the air until someone shares. You can then say, "Thank you. What about others? What came to you when you sat with the passage?"

Group Dynamics

Leading a group through *People Are Asking . . . Is This the End?* will be highly rewarding for both you and your group members—but that doesn't mean you will not encounter any challenges along the way! Discussions can get off track. Group members may not be sensitive to the needs and ideas of others. Some might worry they will be expected to talk about matters that make them feel awkward. Others may express comments that result in disagreements. To help ease this strain on you and the group, consider the following ground rules:

- When someone raises a question or comment that is off the main topic, suggest you deal with it another time, or, if you feel led to go in that direction, let the group know you will be spending some time discussing it.

- If someone asks a question you don't know how to answer, admit it and move on. At your discretion, feel free to invite group members to comment on questions that call for personal experience.

- If you find one or two people are dominating the discussion time, direct a few questions to others in the group. Outside the main group time, ask the more dominating members to help you draw out the quieter ones. Work to make them a part of the solution instead of the problem.

- When a disagreement occurs, encourage the group members to process the matter in love. Encourage those on opposite sides to restate what they heard the other side say about the matter, and then invite each side to evaluate if that perception is accurate. Lead the group in examining other Scriptures related to the topic and look for common ground.

When any of these issues arise, encourage your group members to follow the words from the Bible: "Love one another" (John 13:34), "If it is possible, as far as it depends on you, live at peace with everyone" (Romans 12:18), and "Be quick to listen, slow to speak and slow to become angry" (James 1:19).

About
Dr. David Jeremiah and Turning Point

D r. David Jeremiah is the founder of Turning Point, a ministry committed to providing Christians with sound Bible teaching relevant to today's changing times through radio and television broadcasts, audio series, books, and live events. Dr. Jeremiah's common-sense teaching on topics such as family, prayer, worship, angels, and biblical prophecy forms the foundation of Turning Point.

David and his wife, Donna, reside in El Cajon, California, where he serves as the senior pastor of Shadow Mountain Community Church. David and Donna have four children and twelve grandchildren.

In 1982, Dr. Jeremiah brought the same solid teaching to San Diego television that he shares weekly with his congregation. Shortly thereafter, Turning Point expanded its ministry to radio. Dr. Jeremiah's inspiring messages can now be heard worldwide on radio, television, and the Internet.

Because Dr. Jeremiah desires to know his listening audience, he travels nationwide holding ministry rallies and spiritual enrichment conferences that touch the hearts and lives of many people. According to Dr. Jeremiah, "At some point in time, everyone reaches a turning point; and for every person, that moment is unique, an experience to hold onto forever. There's so much changing in today's world that sometimes it's difficult to choose the right path. Turning Point offers people an understanding of God's Word as well as the opportunity to make a difference in their lives."

Dr. Jeremiah has authored numerous books, including *Escape the Coming Night* (Revelation), *The Handwriting on the Wall* (Daniel), *Overcoming Loneliness, Prayer—The Great Adventure, God in You* (Holy Spirit), *When Your World Falls Apart, My Heart's Desire, 31 Days to Happiness—Searching for Heaven on Earth, Captured by Grace, Grace Givers, Signs of Life, What in the World Is Going On?, The Coming Economic Armageddon, I Never Thought I'd See the Day!, God Loves You: He Always Has—He Always Will, What Are You Afraid Of?, Agents of the Apocalypse,* and *RESET—Ten Steps to Spiritual Renewal.*

Stay Connected to Dr. David Jeremiah

Take advantage of two great ways to let Dr. David Jeremiah give you spiritual direction every day! Both are absolutely FREE.

Turning Points Magazine and Devotional

Receive Dr. David Jeremiah's magazine, *Turning Points*, each month:

- Thematic study focus
- 48 pages of life-changing reading
- Relevant articles
- Special features
- Daily devotional readings
- Bible study resource offers
- Live event schedule
- Radio & television information

Daily Turning Point E-Devotional

Start your day off right! Find words of inspiration and spiritual motivation waiting for you on your computer every morning! Receive a daily e-devotion communication from David Jeremiah that will strengthen your walk with God and encourage you to live the authentic Christian life.

There are two easy ways to sign up for these free resources from Turning Point. Visit us online at www.DavidJeremiah.org and select "Subscribe to Daily Devotional by Email" or visit the home page and find Daily Devotional to subscribe to your monthly copy of *Turning Points*.

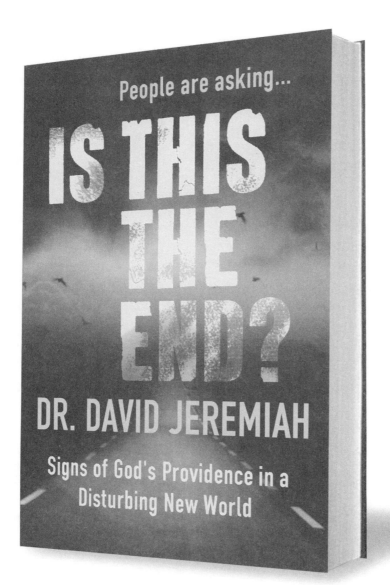

AVAILABLE WHEREVER BOOKS ARE SOLD

For more information and resources,
please visit IsThisTheEnd.com.